THE
COLLEGE BRED
NEGRO AMERICAN

Report of a Social Study made by Atlanta University under the patronage of the Trustees of the John F. Slater Fund; with the Proceedings of the 15th Annual Conference for the Study of the Negro Problems, held at Atlanta University, on Tuesday, May 24th, 1910

Edited by

W. E. Burghardt Du Bois, Ph.D.
Director of Publicity and Research, National Association for the Advancement of Colored People

and

Augustus Granville Dill, A.M.
Associate Professor of Sociology in Atlanta University

ISBN: 978-1-63923-852-1

Printed: March 2023

Published and Distributed By:
Lushena Books
607 Country Club Drive, Unit E
Bensenville, IL 60106
www.lushenabks.com

ISBN: 978-1-63923-852-1

ALL that a man does outwardly is but the expression and completion of his inward thot. To work effectually, he must think clearly; to act nobly, he must think nobly. Intellectual force is a principal element of the soul's life, and should be proposed by every man as the principal end of his being.

—*Channing.*

The College=bred Negro American

Contents

The Fifteenth Annual Conference

The Higher Education of Negro Americans

PROGRAM ·

First Session, 10:00 a. m.
(Ware Memorial Chapel)

President E. T. Ware presiding.
Subject: "Relation of Higher Education to Other Kinds of Training."
Address: President J. H. Dillard of the Jeanes Fund.

Second Session, 11:30 a. m.

Subject: "Education and Health."
For women: Ware Memorial Chapel.
For men: Room 13, Stone Hall.

Third Session, 3:15 p. m.

Thirteenth Annual Mothers' Meeting. (In charge of the Gate City Free
Kindergarten Association.) Mrs. David T. Howard presiding.
Subject: "The Education of the Child."

1. Kindergarten songs, games and exercises by 125 children of the five free kindergartens.
2. Address: Report of the year's work in each school—Mrs. John Rush.
3. Explanation of Kindergarten Exhibit—Miss Minetta Sammis.
4. Report of Treasurer—Mrs. Lizzie Burch.
5. Collection.

Fourth Session, 8:00 p. m.

President E. T. Ware presiding.
Subject: "The College-bred Negro American."
Short addresses by presidents and representatives of Negro colleges.
Stereopticon exhibit of Higher Education.

Special Sessions
(Suite 16, Stone Hall. Admission by invitation only.)

8:00-10:00 a. m.

"Methods and Results of the Present Investigation." Dr. DuBois, of
Atlanta University, in charge.

11:00 a. m.-1:00 p. m.

"The Need and Supply of Negro College Students." President Kumler,
of Walden University, presiding.

1:30-3:30 p. m.

"The Curriculum of Negro Colleges." President Gates, of Fisk University, presiding.

4:00-6:00 p. m.

"The Financial Support of Negro Colleges." President Dunton, of Claflin
University, presiding.

Preface

In 1900 the Atlanta University Negro Conference made an investigation of the college graduates among Negro Americans. The study received widespread publicity and did much towards clearing up misapprehension in regard to educated colored people.

Ten years later we return to the same investigation aided by an appropriation of $1,000 from the Trustees of the John F. Slater Fund. The results are based on college catalogs, letters of officials and the reports of 800 Negro graduates. This is, therefore, far from an exhaustive study, but it has much value.

This study is, therefore, a further carrying out of the Atlanta University plan of social study of the Negro American, by means of an annual series of decennially recurring subjects covering, so far as is practicable, every phase of human life. The object of these studies is primarily scientific—a careful research for truth, conducted as thoroly, broadly and honestly as the material resources and mental equipment at command will allow. It must be remembered that mathematical accuracy in these studies is impossible; the sources of information are of varying degrees of accuracy and the pictures are wofully incomplete. There is necessarily much repetition in the successive studies, and some contradiction of previous reports by later ones as new material comes to hand. All we claim is that the work is as thoro as circumstances permit and that with all its obvious limitations it is well worth the doing. Our object is not simply to serve science. We wish not only to make the truth clear but to present it in such shape as will encourage and help social reform.

Our financial resources are unfortunately meager: Atlanta University is primarily a school and most of its funds and energy go to teaching. It is, however, also a seat of learning and as such it has endeavored to advance knowledge, particularly in matters of racial contact and development, which

seem obviously its nearest field.   In this work it has received
unusual encouragement from the scientific world, and the published results of these studies are used in America, Europe,
Asia and Africa.   Very few books on the Negro problem, or
any phase of it, have been published in the last decade which
have not acknowledged their indebtedness to our work.

On the other hand, the financial support given this work
has been very small.   The total cost of the fifteen publications has been about $17,000, or a little over $1,000 a year.
The growing demands of the work, the vast field to be covered
and the delicacy and equipment needed in such work, call for
far greater resources.   We need, for workers, laboratory and
publications, a fund of $6,000 a year, if this work is going
adequately to fulfill its promise.   Three years ago a small
temporary grant from the Carnegie Institution of Washington,
D. C., greatly helped us; and for three years our work has
been saved from suspension by an appropriation from the John
F. Slater Fund.

In past years we have been enabled to serve the United
States Bureau of Labor, the United States Census, the Board
of Education of the English Government, many scientific associations, professors in nearly all the leading universities, and
many periodicals and reviews.   May we not hope in the future
for such increased financial resources as will enable us to study
adequately this the greatest group of social problems that ever
faced America?

Resolutions of the Fifteenth Atlanta Conference

1. There is an increased and pressing demand for college trained Negroes.

2. The Negro graduates are at present, with few exceptions, usefully and creditably employed.

3. The course of study in these colleges does not call for any peculiar modification, but should, on the whole, conform to the general type of curriculum designed for the preparation of broadly educated men to take their places in modern civilization.

4. There should be at least one college for Negro students in each state, liberally endowed.

5. There should be every effort towards co-operation between colleges in the same locality, and towards avoidance of unnecessary duplication of work.

6. We believe that Negro public high schools in the South are greatly needed.

7. We believe in perfect honesty in living up to catalog requirements of admission.

8. We believe the amount of Greek and Latin in college should be gradually reduced.

9. We believe that time given to Natural Science, English, History and Sociology should be increased.

10. We believe that vocational training is a pressing need of Negroes but that it should be preceded by as much cultural training as possible.

President John Hope, Atlanta Baptist College.
President E. T. Ware, Atlanta University.
Dr. W. E. B. DuBois, Atlanta University.
Prof. B. W. Valentine, Benedict College.
President W. E. Holmes, Central City College.
President L. M. Dunton, Claflin University.
President W. H. Crogman, Clark University.
President George A. Gates, Fisk University.
Dean L. B. Moore, Howard University.
Mr. H. S. Dunbar, Paine College.
President Lucy Hale Tapley, Spelman Seminary.
President J. M. P. Metcalf, Talladega College.
Rev. A. W. Partch, Tougaloo University.
President John Kumler, Walden University.
Chaplain T. G. Stewart, Wilberforce University.

A Select Bibliography of Higher Education for Negro Americans

Part I

Arranged alphabetically by authors

Archer, William. Through Afro-America. New York, 1910.

Atlanta University Publications, The. The College-bred Negro. Atlanta, 1900 (1902), 115 (33) pp. 8vo.

Beard, A. F. A Crusade of Brotherhood. Boston and New York, 1909. 334 pp.

Brousseau, Kate. L' education des Negres aux Etats Unis. Paris, 1904. xvi, 396 (1) pp. 8vo.

Bruce, Roscoe Conkling. Service by the Educated Negro. Tuskegee, 1903, 17 pp. 12mo.

Bumstead, Horace. Higher Education of the Negro—its practical Value. Atlanta, 1870. 15 pp. 24 mo.

Corey, Chas. H. A History of the Richmond Theological Seminary. Richmond, 1895. 240 pp. 12mo.

Crummell, Alexander. The attitude of the American mind toward the Negro intellect. Washington, 1898. 12 pp.

Curry, J. L. M. Difficulties, complications and limitations connected with the education of the Negro. Baltimore, 1895. 23 pp. 8vo. J. F. Slater Fund papers.

Curry, J. L. M. Education of Negroes since 1860. Baltimore, 1890. 32 pp. 8vo. J. F. Slater fund papers.

Douglass, H. P. Christian Reconstruction in the South. Boston, 1909. 407 pp.

DuBois, W. E. B. The Souls of Black Folk. Chicago, 1903. viii (1), 264 (1) pp. 8vo.

Easton, Hosea. A treatise on the intellectual character and condition of the colored people of the United States. Boston, 1837. 54 pp. 8vo.

Eaton, John. Report of freedmen's schools for 1864-1865. (Contained in report of the General Superintendent of Freedmen. Department of the states of Tennessee and Arkansas. 1864-5.)

Goodwin, M. B. History of schools for the colored population in the District of Columbia. U. S. Bureau of Education. Special report on District of Columbia for 1869. Pp. 193-300.

Gregoire, H. Enquiry concerning the intellectual and moral faculties, etc., of Negroes. Brooklyn, 1810. 253 pp. 8vo.

Hartshorn, W. N. An Era of Progress and Promise. Boston, 1910. 576 pp.

Haygood, Atticus Green. Our Brother in Black, etc. New York, 1881. 252 pp. 12mo.

Haygood, Atticus Green. The case of the Negro, as to education in the southern states, etc. Atlanta, 1885. 59 pp. 8vo.

Lovinggood, R. S. Why *hic, haec, hoc* for the Negro? Marshall, Tex., 1900. 56 pp. 16 mo.

Mayo, Amory Dwight. How shall the colored youth of the South be educated? Boston, 1897. (1), 213-224 pp. 8vo.

Mayo, Amory Dwight. Northern and Southern women in the education of the Negro in the South. U. S. Bureau of Education. Circular of Information, No. 1, p. 71. 1892.

Mayo, Amory Dwight. The opportunity and obligation of the educated class of the colored people in the Southern states. N. p., 1899 (?). 32 pp. 8vo.

Miller, Kelly. Race Adjustment. New York and Washington, 1908. 306 pp.

Miller, Kelly. The Education of the Negro. Washington, 1902. U. S. Bureau of Education Reports, 1900-01. Vol. I, pp. 731-859. '

Mitchell, E. C. Higher Education and the Negro. N. p., 1896. 19 pp. 12mo.

Negro Young People's Christian and Educational Congress, Atlanta, 1902. 600 pp. 8vo. The United Negro. Atlanta, 1902.

Richings, G. F. Evidences of Progress among Colored People. ——, 1896.

United States Bureau of Education. Education of the colored race. Negroes in America. Washington, 1896. (In report of Commissioner for 1893-94. Vol. I, 1038-1061 pp.)

United States Bureau of Education. Education of the colored race. Washington, 1901. Report 1899-1900.

United States Bureau of Education. Education of the colored race. Washington, 1902. Report 1900-1901.

Wright, Richard R. Brief Historical Sketch of Negro Education in Georgia. Savannah, Ga., 1894. 58 pp. 8vo.

Part II. Periodical Literature

American Journal of Social Science:
Higher education of Negroes. H. L. Wayland. 34:68.
Present problem of the education of Negroes. W. H. Baldwin. 37:52.
Education of Negroes. C. D. Warner. 38:1.
Education of Negroes. K. Miller. 39:117.

American Negro Academy: Occasional Papers.
No. 3. (a) Civilization the primal need of the race. (b) The attitude of the American mind toward the Negro intellect. Alexander Crummell.
No. 8. The educated Negro and his mission. W. S. Scarborough.

Atlantic:
Education of Negroes. W. T. Harris. 69:721.

Training of black men. W. E. B. DuBois. 90:289-97.

Charities Review:
Atlanta University Conferences. W. E. B. DuBois. 10:435.

Dial:
Function of the Negro college. K. Miller. 32:267.

Education:
Education of Negroes. C. G. Andrews. 6:221.
Training of the Negro teacher. N. B. Young. 21:359.

Educational Review:
Education of the Negro in its historical aspects. D. L. Kiehle. 27:299.

Forum:
Negro and higher learning. W. S. Scarborough. 33,349.

Gunton's Magazine:
Atlanta: the center of Negro education of the world. M. G. Anderson. 25:433-41.

Independent:
Negro graduates. 53:1147-8.
Education of white and black. E. A. Alderman. 53:2647-9.
Higher education for the colored youth. A. F. Hilger. 54:1500-2.

Missionary Review:
What intellectual training is doing for the Negro. W. E. B. DuBois. 27:578-82.

Nation:
Education of Negroes of the South. 24:276.
Higher education for the colored youth. 74:381.
South and the educated Negro. 76:324.
Educated Negro and the South. 78:143.

National Quarterly Review:
Intellectual position of the Negro. R. T. Greener. 41:164.

New England Magazine:
Education of Negroes. A. D. Mayo. 17:213.

North American Review:
Education and civilization of freedmen. E. E. Hale. 101:528.
Negro intellect. W. Matthew. 149:91.
Will education solve the race problem? J. R. Straton. 170:785-801.

Outlook:
Training of Negroes for social power. W. E. B. DuBois. 75:409-14.

Popular Science Monthly:
Higher education for the colored youth. A. F. Hilger. 57:437-8.

Slater Fund, Proceedings and Occasional Papers of the:
No. 3. Curry: Education of Negroes since 1860.
No. 5. Curry: Difficulties connected with education of Negroes.

Southern Literary Messenger:
Capabilities of Negroes. W. H. Holcombe. 33:401.

Spectator:
Capacity of Negroes. 75:927.

THE COLLEGE=BRED NEGRO

Section 1. Scope of the Inquiry

In 1900 Atlanta University made a study of the colored colleges in the United States and colored graduates of them and other colleges. Ten years later we come back to the same study, made essentially on the same plan.

The first work was to determine which of the Negro institutions were to be considered colleges. This was done by testing the entrance requirements of these institutions according to the "Carnegie units," i. e. the units of work laid down by the Carnegie Foundation for the Advancement of Teaching.

The next work was to correspond with the colleges of the land and find out the number of colored graduates. This gave only approximate results as the color was not always a matter of record.

Finally a list of living colored college graduates was obtained and a blank with the following questions was sent them.

DEAR SIR or MADAME:

The Atlanta University Conference is repeating this year the inquiry made into the work and condition of college-bred Negro Americans, which it made first in 1900. This study was used, quoted and read all over the world, and the present study will be equally in demand.

I ask your earnest and prompt co-operation. Please fill out and return the enclosed blank immediately. All answers are strictly confidential.

THE COLLEGE-BRED NEGRO AMERICAN, 1910

1. No . .   2. Sex . .   .   3. Address .   .   .   . .
4. Born in (State and place)   . . . . .   in the year .   . .
5. Single, married, widowed or divorced .   ; year of marriage . .   . .
6. Number of children: living .   ; dead (including still born)
7. Early life and training.
8. Education (school, college, professional school, etc.)
9. Honorary degrees.
10. Occupation since graduation, with terms of service.
11. Membership in learned societies.
12. Publications: Essays and books.
13. Public offices held, and political activity.
14. Activity in charitable work and work of social reform.
15. Amount of land owned.
16. Assessed value of real estate, land and houses.

17. Total property owned (market value—confidential).
18. How shall you educate your children?
19. What have been your chief hinderances?
20. Briefly, what is your present practical philosophy in regard to the Negro race in America?   (

About 800 answers to these blanks were received.

Section 2. The Negro College

The first annual report of the President and Treasurer of the Carnegie Foundation for the Advancement of Teaching lays down the following standard requirements for admission to college: at least fourteen units, "a unit being a course of five periods weekly throughout the academic year of the preparatory school. For the purposes of the Foundation the units in each branch of academic study have also been quantitatively defined, the aim being to assign values to the subjects in accordance with the time usually required to prepare adequately upon them for college entrance."

The fourth annual report suggests as a statement that a unit "represents a year's study in any subject in a secondary school, constituting approximately a quarter of a full year's work." This statement assumes "a well ordered high school course" and "limits to four units the amount of credit possible to attain within a given year."

In accordance with this we may arrange the following tables of Negro colleges. In these tables students are graded according to work done. If, for instance, a student has finished the 12th grade and is studying regularly in the institution he is counted as Freshman College, altho he may be in the Normal school. Professional students are not included in these tables.

FIRST GRADE COLORED COLLEGES

(14 or more units of entrance requirements and more than 20 students of college rank).

1.	Howard	. 238	7.	Clark .	35
2.	Fisk . .	. 117	8.	Knoxville .	29
3.	Atlanta	78	9.	Spelman . .	27
4.	Wiley . .	50	10.	Claflin .	23
5.	Leland . . .	43	11.	Atlanta Baptist	22
6.	Virginia Union .	36			

SECOND GRADE COLORED COLLEGES

(12 to 14 units of entrance requirements and over 20 students).

12. Lincoln . . . 132
13. Talladega . 30
14. Wilberforce 19

OTHER COLORED COLLEGES

(A) Those with 14 or more units of entrance requirements, but 20 or fewer students.

15. Lane	20	21. Bennett .	13
16. G. R. Smith . .	20	22. Morgan	10
17. State, Louisville,		23. Straight . .	9
Ky.	18	24. Lincoln Institute .	4
18. Bishop .	18	25. Hartshorn . . .	3
19. Walden . .	16	26. Miles Memorial	2
20. New Orleans .	15		

(B) Those with less than 12 units of entrance requirements and more than 20 students.

27. Shaw . . . 51
28. Benedict . 36

(C) Colleges with less than 12 units of entrance requirements and few college students.

29. Morris Brown . . . 20	31. Langston	6
30. Paine . 7	32. So. Carolina State . 3

To these we may append the rank of the best industrial schools:

9-12 units.

Kentucky (Frankfort)   Princess Anne (Md.)
A. & M. College (N. C.)   Prairie View (Tex.)
Hampton (Va.)   Institute (W. Va.)
Tallahassee (Fla.)

4-6 units.

Tuskegee (Ala.)   Pine Bluff (Ark.)

The standard of the leading colored colleges, as shown in the above groupings, may be compared with that of the leading white colleges of the South.

Institution	Requirements for admission in units, 1907-8[1]
University of North Carolina .	14.7
West Virginia University	14.3
Randolph-Macon College .	14
Trinity College . . .	14
University of Georgia .	12
University of Virginia . .	11.5[2]
University of South Carolina .	11.2
Washington and Lee University	11
University of Alabama	10.5
Roanoke College .	7.5

[1]Third Annual Report of the President and Treasurer of the Carnegie Foundation, pp. 92, 93.   [2]In 1909, 14.5 units.

The date of founding and the number of students in Negro colleges appear in the following table. Where there are several courses, such as college, normal, academic, etc., the students are all classified according to the grade of work which is being done:

1909—

TABLE GIVING DATE OF ESTABLISHMENT OF COLLEGE DEPT.,

INSTITUTION	LOCATION	Date of establishment of college department	Number students in college classes							Number students in high school					
			Graduate	Senior	Junior	Sophomore	Freshman	Special	Total	12th	11th	10th	9th	Special	Total
1. Miles Memorial College	Birmingham, Ala.	1907			1		1		2	1	11	12	14		38
2. Talladega College	Talladega, Ala.	1885		7	6	7	5	5	30	18	12	31	55		116
3. Howard University	Washington, D. C.	1868	1	35	35	46	82	39	238	46	58	113	167	18	402
4. Atlanta Baptist College	Atlanta, Ga.	1890		2	8	7	5		22	14	10	9	23		56
5. Atlanta University	Atlanta, Ga.	1872	2	6	10	15	43	2	78	35	48	70	145		298
6. Morris Brown College	Atlanta, Ga.	1894				8	12		20	28	31	37	49		145
7. Spelman Seminary	Atlanta, Ga.	1897			1	2	12	12	27	11	12	26	56		105
8. Paine College	Augusta, Ga.	1888			3	1	3		7	21	28	29	30		108
9. Clark University	South Atlanta, Ga.	1879		4	8	2	21		35	9	29	43	71		152
10. State University	Louisville, Ky.			2	2		13	1	18	12	18	27	43		100
11. Leland University	New Orleans, La.	1870	24	4	3	2	10		43	15	9	15	31		70
12. New Orleans University	New Orleans, La.	1874		5	2	1	7		15	10	19	33	63		125
13. Straight University	New Orleans, La.	1869	4				5		9	12	9	15	40	10	86
14. Morgan College	Baltimore, Md.	1884				3	2	5	10	17	16	15	19		67
15. Lincoln Institute	Jefferson City, Mo.	1890				2	2		4	57	49	36	71		213
16. Geo. R. Smith College*	Sedalia, Mo.	1898					5	15	20	20	38	28	45	6	137
17. Bennett College	Greensboro, N. C.					5	3	5	13	8	14	16	29		67
18. Shaw University*	Raleigh, N. C.	1870			8	11	18	14	51	16			27		43
19. Wilberforce University	Wilberforce, O.	1856	a												
20. Col. A. & M. College*	Langston, Okla.				2	1	3		6	2	8	22	26	4	62
21. Lincoln University	Lincoln Univ., Pa.	1864		28	30	45	29		132						
22. Benedict College	Columbia, S. C.	1894	2	5	4	12	13		36	48	40	61	32		181
23. Claflin University	Orangeburg, S. C.	1878		6	1	1	15		23	42	40	52	56	24b	214
24. S. C. State College	Orangeburg, S. C.	1896					3		3	24	32	39	43		138
25. Lane College	Jackson, Tenn.	1900		2	3	6	9		20	25	6	19	44	1	95
26. Knoxville College	Knoxville, Tenn.	1877		5	4	9	11		29	29	24	36	32	25	146
27. Fisk University	Nashville, Tenn.	1871	6	20	28	20	43		117	42	47	39	58	1	187
28. Walden University	Nashville, Tenn.	1873		3	3		7	3	16	17	18	29	76	19	159
29. Bishop College	Marshall, Tex.			4	4	4	6		18	18	23	25	55		121
30. Wiley University	Marshall, Tex.			11	9	13	17		50	19	35	35	34	2	125
31. Hartshorn Mem. Col.	Richmond, Va.	1892		1	1	1			3	3	5	8	15		31
32. Virginia Union Univ.	Richmond, Va.	1898	1	8	5	8	14		36	23	23	42	21		109
Total			40	162	189	245	432	64	1131	642	722	962	1470	110	3896

*Catalog 1908-9.

aExact information unobtainable.

bIncluding 7 taking "Special Courses" and 17 in Business College (Catalog p. 79).

—1910

WITH THE NUMBER OF STUDENTS BY CLASSES AND GRADES

	Number students in grades										Profes-sional	Indus-trial	Music	Total in whole school
	8th	7th	6th	5th	4th	3rd	2nd	1st	Special	Total				
	21	33	24	38	20	18	13	12	70c	179	28		49	268
	38	54	57	75	73	73	72	42		554				728
											592			1232
	25	26	31	24					1	107	38			223
														376
	41	52	62	84	81	77	79	85		561	39			765
	45	59	64	89	51	54	40	25	16d	443	28	43	2	648
	35	41	37	18	15				1	147	16			278
	48	55	54	41	27	32	13	11	9	290				477
	21	11								32	8			158
	17	44	32	40	48	16	7	4	2	210	26			349
	38	34	64	55	59	44	29	37	22e	382	2	1		525
	39	43	72	85	79	96	56	58	20f	548			6	649
														77
l	72	34	43	10					29	188				405
	22	15	2	5	2	1				47				204
	28	29	53		21	9	2	8		150				230
	69	69	75	29						242	206	19	4	565
	67	45	42	115					4	273		26		367
											62			194
	44	52	94	31	45	40	26	41		373	57			647
	48	48	57	71	81	73	23	7	103g	511				748
	50	92	88	81	79	65				455		6		602
	24	50	53							127	42			284
	38	28	35	24	38	17	6	11		197	8	29		409
	11	14	13	12	12	8	10	9		89		13	51	457
	45	32	19	18						114	402	2		693
	54	34	22							110				249
	54	54	61	65	42	30			35	341	22			538
	28	23	32	39					3	125				159
	21	29								50	26			221
	1043	1100	1186	1049	773	653	376	350	315	6845	1602	139	112	13725

cThirty-five in night schools and 35 in kindergarten.
dStudents in night school.
eStudents in night school.
fStudents in kindergarten.
gIn afternoon free school.

PROPORTION OF TOTAL COLLEGE TIME
DEVOTED TO DIFFERENT STUDIES

ATLANTA
FISK
ATLANTA BAPTIST
HOWARD
SPELMAN
CLARK
STRAIGHT
LANE
VIRGINIA UNION
NEW ORLEANS
WALDEN
BISHOP
TALLADEGA
CLAFLIN
MORGAN
WILEY
GEO. R. SMITH
BENNETT

1. ANCIENT LANGUAGES
2. MODERN LANGUAGES
3. NATURAL SCIENCES
4. MATHEMATICS
5. ENGLISH
6. SOCIOLOGY AND HISTORY
7. PHILOSOPHY
8. MISCELLANEOUS

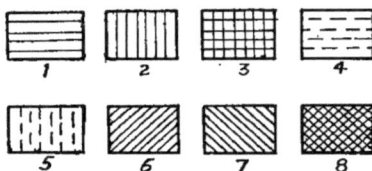

As has been shown, there are about thirty-two colored institutions doing college work; but the leading colleges, according to the Carnegie Foundation units, which have a reasonable number of students are:

Howard University	Knoxville College
Fisk University	Spelman Seminary
Atlanta University	Claflin University
Wiley University	Atlanta Baptist College
Leland University	Lincoln University
Virginia Union University	Talladega College
Clark University	

In addition to their college work, nine of these institutions are carrying on work in one or more of the professional departments. These are Howard, Wiley, Leland, Virginia Union, Knoxville, Spelman, Atlanta Baptist College, Lincoln and Talladega. And almost all of them are doing work also in the High School or Academy—which work corresponds to "College Preparatory." Because of this latter fact, adverse criticism has often been pronounced against these institutions of higher learning. These institutions have been accused of going under the name of *college* when so much of their work was actual high school work. A more careful study of educational conditions in the South, however, would present the case in a different light. To be sure, much of the energy of these institutions has been devoted to training in high school branches; but this has been absolutely necessary. The South has been slow in providing public high schools for the education of her Negro children and even today comparatively little is being done in that direction. The report of the United States Commissioner of Education for the year ending July, 1909, showed that in the whole South there were but one hundred and twelve public high schools for Negroes. Even the larger cities which provide something of primary and grammar school education for Negroes make little or no provision for their high school training. The results here are two: first, Negro children graduating from the grammar school are unable to find public instruction in high school work; and second, the Negro colleges are without public feeders.   To meet this situation the Negro colleges have been compelled to provide in large part their own feeders.   The rise of the Negro secondary schools thruout the South, for the most part established and directed by graduates of these higher institutions and supported by voluntary contributions, has been of great help in this direction.   To insure the best and largest results in the future the South must take a more liberal view of public education for Negroes.

To find the predominant character of these institutions we may make the following table:

INSTITUTION	Total	Profes-sional	College	All other students	Total college and lower students	Per cent of college to college and lower students
Howard . .	1232	592	238	402	640	37.2
Fisk . .	457	. .	117	340	457	25.6
Atlanta .	376	. . .	78	298	376	20.7
Wiley .	538	22	50	466	516	9.6
Leland	349	26	43	280	323	13.3
Virginia Union	221	26	36	159	195	18.4
Clark . .	477	. .	35	442	477	7.3
Knoxville .	409	8	29	372	401	7.2
Spelman . .	648	28	27	593	620	4.3
Claflin	748	. .	23	725	748	3.07
Atlanta Baptist . .	223	38	22	163	185	11.8
Lincoln . . .	194	62	132	. . . .	194	68.04
Talladega .	728	28	30	670	700	4.2

By giving the per cent of college students to total college and lower students the preceding table also shows with some considerable degree of accuracy what share of each institution's work is being devoted to college training.

In order to determine the grade of college students more carefully we may make the following table of Negro institutions doing college work.   This table is based upon the catalogs of the various institutions, those of 1909-10 being used in almost all cases, and shows the ·distribution of students of college rank by grade and class. The table is as follows:

1909=1910
Number of Students of College Rank According to Catalog

INSTITUTION	Graduate	Senior	Junior	Soph.	Fresh.	Special	Others of college rank	Total
1. Miles Memorial College	.	.	1	.	1	.	.	2
2. Talladega College	.	7	6	7	5	5	.	30
3. Howard University	1	23	30	38	53	4	89	238
4. Atlanta University	2	6	10	15	20	2	23	78
5. Atlanta Baptist College	.	2	8	7	5	.	.	22
6. Morris Brown College	.	.	8	10	7	.	2	27
7. Spelman Seminary	.	1	2	.	3	.	21	27
8. Paine College	.	3	1	3	8	.	.	15
9. Clark University	.	4	8	2	14	.	7	35
10. State University (Kentucky)	.	2	2	.	.	• 1	13	18
11. Leland University	24	4	3	2	7	.	3	43
12. New Orleans University	.	5	2	1	7	.	.	15
13. Straight University	4	.	.	.	.	.	5	9
14. Morgan College	.	.	3	2	5	.	.	10
15. Lincoln Institute	.	.	2	.	2	.	.	4
16. Geo. R. Smith College*	.	.	.	.	5	15	.	20
17. Bennett College	.	.	.	5	3	5	.	13
18. Shaw University*	.	8	11	18	16	14	.	67
19. Colored A. & M. College*	.	.	2	.	.	2	2	6
20. Lincoln University	.	28	30	45	29	.	.	132
21. Benedict College	2	5	4	12	13	.	.	36
22. Claflin University	.	6	1	1	15	.	.	23
23. South Carolina State College	.	3	.	.	.	.	.	3
24. Lane College	.	2	3	6	9	.	.	20
25. Knoxville College	.	5	4	9	11	.	.	29
26. Fisk University	6	20	28	20	17	.	26	117
27. Walden University	.	3	.	8	7	3	.	16
28. Bishop College	.	4	4	4	6	.	.	18
29. Wiley University	.	11	9	13	17	.	.	50
30. Hartshorn Memorial College	.	1	1	1	.	.	.	3
31. Virginia Union University	1	8	5	8	14	.	.	36

* Catalog 1908-9.

Section 3. Curricula in Negro Colleges

The studies in Negro colleges can best be illustrated by the following schedule which shows also the general division of time between these subjects. The diagram which appears on page 16 is a graphic presentation of the proportion of the total college time (i. e. the total recitation time of a full college course) devoted by these institutions to the different studies:

Comparison of college studies, number of hours devoted to each (by classes),

		Virginia Union Hours	V.U. Per cent of total college time	Lane Hours	Lane Per cent	Straight Hours	Straight Per cent	Clark Hours	Clark Per cent	Spelman Hours	Spelman Per cent	Howard Hours	Howard Per cent	Atlanta Baptist Col. Hours	A.B.C. Per cent	Fisk Hours	Fisk Per cent	Atlanta Hours	Atlanta Per cent
Ancient Languages	Senior		10.1	180	23.2	192	22.9	128	31.6	256	21	102	14.7	256	19	198	21.7	186	19.1
	Junior	256		180		256		288		256		102		256		288		306	
	Sophomore			360				288				102							
	Freshman																		
Modern Languages	Senior	128	9.4	90	8.7	64	9.8	128	11.5	128	5.2	102	9.8	128	9.5	90	12	170	13.2
	Junior	112		180		128		128				102		128		180		136	
	Sophomore																		
	Freshman																		
Natural Sciences	Senior	160	13.9	180	20.3	128	13.9	96	16.8	192	15.7	102	14.7	192	14.2	180	17.7	102	16.1
	Junior	192		180		48		128		64		102				90		186	
	Sophomore			90		96		128		128		102				126		136	
	Freshman			180															
Mathematics	Senior	80	9.4	180	20.3	64	9.8	96	11.5	64	7.8	102	9.8	64	7.1	180	8	68	8.8
	Junior	160		270		128		160		128		102		128				186	
	Sophomore			180															
	Freshman																		
English	Senior	96	16.1	36	3.4	128	9.8	96	7.1	64	11.8	102	14.7	64	10.7	180	12	170	13.2
	Junior	96		72		64		160		128		102		128		54			
	Sophomore	96								64		102		64		36			
	Freshman	96								32				32					
Sociology and Hist.	Senior	160	11.3	90	5.8	224	13.9	112	7.9	128	13.1	102	9.8	128	11.9	180	12.9	186	19.1
	Junior	64		90		48		64		128		102		128		108		306	
	Sophomore									64				64					
	Freshman																		
Philosophy	Senior	160	8.8	486	16.6	176	9	192	14.3	288	17.1	204	14.7	288	15.4	72	7.2	170	10.2
	Junior	64						128		128		102		128		90		68	
	Sophomore																		
	Freshman																		
Miscellaneous	Senior	192	21.5	72	2.3	112	10.6			64	7.8	204	11.4	128	11.9	18	8		
	Junior	96				32				64				128		54			
	Sophomore	128				32				64				64		108			
	Freshman	128				32						34							

per cent of total college time (full college course) devoted to each

For each college two rows are shown: "Per cent of total college time" and "Hours." Within each subject the hour figures run Senior / Junior / Sophomore / Freshman.

College	Measure	Ancient Languages	Modern Languages	Natural Sciences	Mathematics	English	Sociology and Hist.	Philosophy	Miscellaneous
Bennett	Per cent	23.6		19.7	10.5	11.8	13.8	20.3	
Bennett	Hours	270 / 270		120 / 90 / 150 / 90	90 / 150	90 / 90 / 90	90 / 225	330 / 135	
Geo. R. Smith	Per cent	21.2	5.3	15.9	15.9	12.4	5.3	14.1	9.5
Geo. R. Smith	Hours	300 / 300	160	160 / 160 / 160	150 / 150 / 150	200 / 156	100 / 50	300 / 100	220 / 50
Wiley	Per cent	12.7	10.1	19.1	13.3	11.4	13.3	9.5	10.1
Wiley	Hours	160 / 160	128 / 128	128 / 96 / 160 / 96	80 / 160 / 96	96 / 96 / 96	176 / 160	160 / 80	192 / 64
Morgan	Per cent	19.7	20.9	9.8	8.6	14.8	13.5	7.4	4.9
Morgan	Hours	68 / 136 / 204 / 136	238 / 102 / 102 / 136	102 / 102 / 68	102 / 136	68 / 102 / 102 / 136	68 / 102 / 136 / 68	102 / 102	34 / 34 / 34 / 34
Claflin	Per cent	18.7	3.7	20	10	17.5	16.2	10	3.7
Claflin	Hours	150 / 150 / 150	90	150 / 150 / 90 / 90	120 / 120	120 / 120 / 90 / 90	90 / 160 / 150	150 / 90	90
Talladega	Per cent	31.2		17.9	14	8.5	7.8	14	6.2
Talladega	Hours	18 / 144 / 198 / 360		180 / 90 / 144	180 / 144	18 / 126 / 18 / 36	180	324	36 / 36 / 36 / 36
Bishop	Per cent	27.8	7.1	7.1	9.2	7.8	13.5	10	17.1
Bishop	Hours	304 / 320	160	160	80 / 128	96 / 80	144 / 80 / 80	176 / 48	320 / 32 / 32
Walden	Per cent	23.6		19.7	10.5	11.8	13.8	15.1	5.2
Walden	Hours	288 / 288		128 / 96 / 160 / 96	96 / 160	96 / 96 / 96	96 / 240	288 / 80	64 / 64
New Orleans	Per cent	13.1	10.5	19.7	10.5	11.8	13.8	20.3	
New Orleans	Hours	160 / 160	256	128 / 96 / 160 / 96	96 / 160	96 / 96 / 96	96 / 240	352 / 144	

Section 4.   A Personal Evaluation

A student of social and educational conditions among Negroes, who has had opportunity thru frequent visits to form an opinion of the work done in Negro colleges, makes the following tabular statement of his evaluation of some twenty odd institutions:

NAME OF INSTITUTION	Thoroness of work done				Adherence to catalog announcements				Quality of work done
	Excellent	Good	Fair	Poor	Excellent	Good	Fair	Poor	
A. and M. College (N. C.).			X					X	Fair
Arkansas Baptist College . .			X					X	Poor
Atlanta Baptist College . .	X				X				Good
Atlanta University .	X				X				Good
Benedict College . .			X			X			Fair
Bennett College . .				X			X		Poor
Bishop College .		X				X			Good
Claflin University . .		X				X			Fair
Clark University		X				X			Fair
Fisk University . . .	X				X				Good
Georgia State College .			X			X			Fair
Howard University .			X			X			Fair
Knoxville College .	X				X				Good
Lane College			X				X		Fair
Miles Memorial College .			X					X	Poor
Morris Brown College . .				X				X	Poor
New Orleans University			X			X			Fair
Paine College . . .		X				X			Fair
Paul Quinn College .				X			X		Poor
Shaw University			X			X			Fair
South Carolina State College .			X			X			Poor
State University .			X			X			Poor
Straight University . .		X				X			Fair
Tougaloo University		X				X			Good
Walden University . .			X				X		Fair
Wilberforce University .			X			X			Fair
Wiley University .		X					X		Good

Excellent—About 90 to 99 per cent.
Good—About 75 to 89 per cent.
Fair—About 60 to 74 per cent.
Poor—Below 60 per cent.

√   ## Section 5.   The Attitude of other Colleges towards Negro Students

Negroes have attended northern colleges for many years, both as graduate and undergraduate students.   As early as
√ 1826 a Negro was graduated from Bowdoin College and almost every year from that time till today has added to the number of Negro graduates from such schools.   Many of the largest
| and best colleges of the North welcome Negroes to their stu-

dent bodies—a welcome which has been taken advantage of by many young men and women of the Negro race.

The rise in the standard of the Negro college has created, among other desires, the desire for more knowledge; so that each year we find many graduates from the Negro colleges applying for admission to the large colleges of the North— sometimes as graduate, sometimes as undergraduate students. Too, many Negro teachers of the South take advantage of the summer quarter to do further educational work. Harvard, Columbia and the University of Chicago have enrolled many such students.

In collecting data for this study the following letter was sent to officials of other colleges:

MY DEAR SIR:—

Atlanta University is making a study of Negro college graduates similar to one made in 1900. May I ask your co-operation?

1. Can you furnish me the names, class and addresses of such of your graduates as are of Negro descent?

2. In general what has been their success and what is the attitude of the institution and student body toward them?

Some replies are given here:

"Princeton University has never had any graduates of Negro descent."

"The Johns Hopkins University has not yet conferred a degree upon a Negro; none have ever applied for a degree, tho to be sure but two men have studied here."

Wells College, Aurora, N. Y.—"We have never graduated a student of Negro descent."

"We have never had a Negro woman as a student in Bryn Mawr College."

Mills College, California.—"There are no graduates of Negro descent on our rolls."

Rockford, Ill.—"We have never had any graduates of Negro descent from Rockford College."

"We have reason to believe that we have at one time had among the students at Barnard College a girl of Negro descent."

Yale University.—"The success of these graduates has varied considerably. Many of them, such as ——— '04, ——— '03 Law, ——— '96, have made most creditable records in every way. Yale University has never tried to attract Negro students and, on the other hand, has never felt justified in refusing admittance to those who became qualified to enter."

Beloit College, Wisconsin. — "These young people were treated with unfailing courtesy by the faculty and students of the college. Mr. —— was a man of some ability as a speaker, and of fair ability as a student. He has not made much of a record since graduation. Mr. ——, while not a thoro student when in college, is a man of unusually attractive qualities, and was a decided favorite while here. He won a large reputation by his rendering of the part of King Oedipus in Sophocles' drama, Oedipus Tyrannus, and also won the second place in the interstate contest in oratory, including twelve states of the interior. On his return from this triumph he was met by the students of the college and I had the pleasure of seeing them carrying him on their shoulders from the train to the carriage which the students then drew themselves instead of the horses doing it. I have often said that this was a sight that could be seen nowhere excepting in an American college.

"Miss —— was a faithful worker, but had hardly mental power enough for her college work. She was favored by the faculty on account of her handicaps, and was graduated; but her health was not good after graduation and she accomplished nothing before her death."

Leland Stanford University. — "I have never been aware of any hostile attitude on the part of the student body toward Negro students. Of course, we have never had but an occasional Negro student in the University."

Fordham University, New York. — "We have had no applicants for admission from the black race. What we should do were the applicants to come I just cannot say."

St. Vincent College, Beatty, Pennsylvania. — "I cannot tell what the attitude of the student body should be towards Negroes, but we shall not risk a trial of it. Applications are very rare—one during the last four years. We do not think it wise here under the prevailing conditions to accept any distinctively colored students into the college."

Hanover, Indiana—"For obvious reasons we have no colored students in Hanover College."

Park College, Parkville, Mo. — "Never a Negro graduate nor a student. Couldn't do it in Missouri if we wanted to."

Missouri Valley College, Marshall, Mo. — "We have never had any graduates of Negro descent and are not likely to ever have."

Carleton College, Farmington, Mo. — "We have never had any Negro or any person with Negro blood graduate from Carleton College in its history. I have not found a student in the state that would tolerate a Negro in the college. And it is even worse since the Johnson-Jeffries fight."

Tarkio College, Tarkio, Mo. — "We have had one Negro student who spent a year in our Preparatory Department. I do not suppose any other white college in the state would receive a Negro student. This young man remained in the school for a year with credit to himself and the school, was a member of its glee club and never an individual intimated to me any objection to his presence. I regard this as a remarkable experience for a Missouri college."

Greenville College, Illinois. — "There is no attitude either for or against them. We do not have applications from members of the colored race."

Union College, College View, Nebraska. — "We have had several Negro students in the past and accept them in our school at the present time. As far as we are able to judge there has not been much distinction made among our students between the Negro students and the others. It depends very largely upon the student himself how he is received by the student body."

"The University of North Dakota is open to all students of any rank or race who are prepared."

South Dakota State College, Brookings, S. D. — "The attitude towards Negro students is not favorable with the student body."

Simpson College, Indianola, Iowa. — "The sentiment of the students seems to be along the line of being willing to help these students in any way possible and, of course, we are far enough North so that race prejudice is not very manifest."

Occidental College, Los Angeles, Cal. — "So far as I know a Negro applying for admission would receive a cordial welcome from the student body. We have Japanese, Koreans and Chinese, and there is no race prejudice in this school so far as I know. The question has never been raised."

Thiel College, Greenville, Pa. — "Should any apply for admission they would be welcome."

Earlham College, Richmond, Ind. — "So far as I know Negro students here are treated with respect by the student body. We never have many of them and they are not thrown closely with the other students in a social way, but all students are measured by their work whether they are white or colored."

Oskaloosa College, Iowa. — "We have had at various times Negro students who have made excellent records in their class-room work."

Upsala College, Kenilworth, N. J. — "We have had some Negro students and they have been treated with same respect as other students."

Hope College, Holland, Mich. — "Hope College has never been favored with having Negro graduates nor even Negro students. I feel confident, however, that if young men of that blood should present themselves as students they would be kindly treated."

Salina Chautauqua Association, Kansas. — "As far as I know the attitude of the student body towards the Negro student has been in most respects at least the same as their attitude toward other students. Our student body, so far as I know, holds no prejudice against the Negro."

Worcester Polytechnic Institute, Mass. — "There has been one [Negro] student in the Freshman Class this year, and, so far as I have been able to notice, no discrimination of any sort has been made either in his favor or against him by the student body."

Oregon Agricultural College, Corvallis, Oregon. — "There were two Negro students registered during the past year and I understand they have been making very good records. One of the young men in question is very active in certain student enterprises, particularly the Cosmopolitan Club, and is popular with the students generally. The attitude of the student body of the Oregon Agricultural College towards colored students, so far as the writer's observation and experiences are concerned, has been very friendly."

Franklin and Marshall College, Lancaster, Pa. — "I am sure such a student would be well received and have courteous treatment from our student body."

Pittsburg College of the Holy Ghost. — "There was within my recollection a Negro student in the college. Our boys treated him as they did the other boys."

Des Moines College, Iowa. — "There has never been any objection on the part of faculty or students toward the presence of Negro students in our institution."

The University of Nebraska. — "We have had a number of Negro graduates and so far as I know the general student body feels very kindly towards them and towards our Negro undergraduates. On commencement days a Negro usually receives a little more applause than a white boy when he walks over the stage. I presume some things happen in his personal relations with his fellow students that are not entirely pleasant, but they never come to the surface. I doubt if there is a school in the country which is freer from race prejudice than the University of Nebraska."

Section 6.   Negro Alumni of the Colleges of Iowa *(by Prof. Paul S. Peirce)*

So far as the writer has been able to determine, there are thirty-four colored alumni of Iowa colleges and universities and these persons hold some forty degrees taken *in cursu*. Of the thirty-four, twenty-six are males and eight are females; of those receiving more than one degree in Iowa institutions, three are men and two are women (one man holding three degrees).

These alumni are distributed among eleven institutions, the State University claiming eleven of them, Drake University six, Iowa Wesleyan University five, Tabor College three, Iowa State College and Coe College two each, and Grinnell, Cornell, Penn, Amity and Highland Park colleges one each. It is a curious coincidence that no one of these institutions seems to have graduated both colored men and colored women, altho all are co-educational; seven have graduated only men of this race and four only women.

The colored alumnus of Iowa colleges seems to be a phenomenon peculiar to the last three decades, and it is interesting, tho not surprising, to note the progressive increase in the number of graduates from decade to decade: during the first decade (1880-1890) six degrees were conferred upon colored candidates; during the next (1890-1900) thirteen; during the decade just closing twenty-one, that is, more than during both the other two.

Equally interesting and reassuring is the increasing range and diversity of courses pursued. During the first decade law and liberal arts held the whole field (law 2, liberal arts 4); during the second decade law and liberal arts were still in the center of the field, but medicine, agriculture and graduate work have entered (law 4, liberal arts 4, medicine 1, graduate 3 and agriculture 1); while during the last decade no less than seven lines of study were completed by colored men and women (law 3, liberal arts 10, pharmacy 4, medicine, dentistry, agriculture and graduate courses one each). The distribution by courses for the entire period is as follows: liberal arts 18, law 9, graduate 4, pharmacy 4, agriculture 2, medicine 2, dentistry 1.

Geographical Distribution

1. As to place of birth, data were secured from twenty-five of the total thirty-four, some neglecting to reply at all and others, who replied to most questions, omitting the answer to this one. Of those reporting ten were born in Iowa, seven in Missouri, two each in North Carolina and South Carolina and one in each of the following states: Alabama, Texas, Virginia and Nebraska.

2. As to migration, several have lived in more than one state since graduation, but as data concerning such movements are quite incomplete we will simply compare birthplaces with present locations. Of the ten born in Iowa five are now in that state, two in Oklahoma, one in Wyoming, one in Minnesota, and one in Venezuela; of the seven born in Missouri two are in Iowa, two in Mississippi, one in Missouri, one in Alabama and one in Oklahoma; of the two born in North Carolina one is in Illinois and one in Missouri; the native of Virginia is a resident of Iowa; the native

of Texas is in Tennessee; the native of Alabama lives in Texas; the native of Nebraska is in Iowa; and of the two South Carolinians one is in Illinois and the other in Georgia.

3. By way of summary of present location, it may be noted that of the thirty-four, twelve have settled in Iowa, four in Missouri, three each in Oklahoma and Illinois, two each in Mississippi and Tennessee, and one in each of the following: Minnesota, Georgia, Texas, Wyoming, Alabama, Venezuela, District of Columbia; and one died in Liberia.

4. These figures show a pretty even division between the northern states on the one hand and the southern and border states on the other, so far as place of birth is concerned and so far as present location goes. But statistics of birthplace and migration are too fragmentary to warrant very definite conclusions as to movements from the one section to the other.

Age Statistics

1. As to age of graduation some facts are perhaps noteworthy: First, that the average age is earlier for women than for men, that of the former being $21\frac{1}{2}$ and of the latter $22\frac{3}{5}$; second, the average has slightly increased from decade to decade, being 21 years for men and women from 1880-1890, 22 years from 1890-1900 and $22\frac{4}{7}$ from 1900-1910. This increase seems much more noticeable among the men than among the women.

2. As to present age, of the twenty-four reporting sixteen are still under thirty-five and only one is over fifty.

The Family

In view of the fact that so large a proportion of the alumni studied are recent graduates, it is not surprising to find a large proportion of them still unmarried. Of the twenty-six reporting twelve were married—ten men and two women, twelve were single—eight men and four women; one is a widower, and one woman is separated from her husband. That is, about one-half have married and one-half remained single, with a very low percentage of separated. Among the men the percentage of marriages was naturally much greater among graduates of the first two decades, while the proportion of marriages among the women was highest for graduates of the last decade.

Of the thirteen who have been married the average age of marriage was for men 30 years, for women 25 years; of the wives of graduates the average age at marriage was 23 years, and of husbands of graduates (only three reported) the average age at marriage was 35 years.

The total number of children of these marriages was twenty-two, of whom seventeen are living and five dead. These children were distributed among seven of the thirteen marriages, four reporting no children, three reporting one child each, two reporting two children each, three reporting three children each and one reporting six children.

Occupation

The thirty-three living alumni studied are at present distributed among the following pursuits: teachers 8, lawyers 5, clergymen 4, physicians 3, pharmacists 3, homemakers 3, editors 2, students 3, dentists 1, civil service 1, railway service 1, restaurant work 1, parcel message delivery 1 (three duplicates).

In addition it should be noted that nine have previously served as teachers for a longer or shorter period, two have been lawyers, one a book agent, one has run a carpet-cleaning establishment and one has been an editor, while fourteen have never had any other than their present occupation.

Testimony of College Authorities as to Negro Students

Amity College. — "Miss B. was a girl of excellent conduct and good scholarship. Her mother (a widow) is still a resident of College Springs, their home for many years. She was a slave, can not write and reads only a little with difficulty. Her livelihood for herself and children has been earned by hard toil washing and ironing."

Central University. — "I will say that while Negroes are admitted to the college freely, but few have attended and none have graduated. We had one year, 1902-1903, a young woman, a quadroon, who received a prize for highest scholarship in the entire school. That was an unusual experience, however. As a rule our Negro students have not done a high grade of work."

Cornell College. — "We have had but one Negro graduate from Cornell College and he made a very fine record as a student while in college. During his college course he was a member of our base ball team and was elected to membership in one of our literary societies."

Coe College. — "So far as I can learn only two Negroes have graduated from Coe College. One was a good student and gave class poem on commencement day. Unfortunately he is a dwarf physically—a hunchback—and for that reason chiefly, I presume, he has not been able to secure such a position as his scholarship would merit. The other was a student of fair ability and fine athlete (football)."

Des Moines College. — "We have none. Within the last twenty years we have had only two students of that race. Neither of them went beyond the freshman year. Both were good students. One of them is doing an excellent work now as pastor of one of the strongest Negro churches in this city. The other, a young woman, who was with us last year, passed perfect examination in her Latin, a thing that had probably never occurred in that class before."

Highland Park College. — "We have never had but one Negro graduated from the regular college of pharmacy. We have had very few Negroes in the past and two years ago, you will probably remember, we announced that we would not receive Negroes any longer, not that we had anything against the Negro, on the other hand we shall be glad to do anything that we can to further Negro education; but it became humiliating to the Negro and compromising to the school; the students would not sit by them in school and would have no communication with them, and since we had only one or two each quarter, we thot it would be better for all parties concerned to have the Negro seek his education under more favorable circumstances."

Leander Clark College. — "We have had a number of Negro students in past years. Some of them did good, creditable work, and have made useful citizens. We have never had a graduate from any of the departments."

Penn College. — "There has been only one Negro graduate. This one was a student of fair ability. Since graduation she has been teaching and has met with excellent success. We have one Negro woman in school at the present time; she is a fair student, above the average in language courses."

Parsons College. — "We have never had a Negro graduate. To my knowledge no Negro has attended this school."

Tabor College. — "We have reason to be proud of our Negro alumni: Mr. Hightower T. Kealing, A. M., editor of A. M. E. *Review*, Nashville, Tenn.; Mr. Edward L. Blackshear, A. M., principal of Texas State Industrial School at Prairie View, Texas; and the Rev. W. H. Speese, B. L., pastor of A. M. E. church of Brookport, Illinois. These men have all demonstrated their worth and are an honor to our institution."

State University. — "The Negro graduates of this University have varied in point of scholarship widely as have the white alumni. But their average has been quite as high as the general average for all alumni, and among their number have been some of marked superiority. A former teacher of logic here said of one of them that he had never had a keener mind in his class room. And another, Mr. S. Joe Brown, was elected to the local chapter of Phi Beta Kappa."

Appreciation of College Training

All are confident that their college training has benefited them. To this question the response is always a positive *yes*. But two of the number addressed felt that it would have been better if their liberal arts work had been supplemented by some commercial or manual training. The rest believed that no other than the course pursued would have been better for them.

Work of Teachers

No vocation has claimed so many of the Negro graduates of Iowa institutions as teaching, and thru no other channel has the influence of college training reached so far. About one-fourth of the total number are now teachers, and more than one-half have been teachers at some time in their lives. In the aggregate they represent more than one hundred and thirty years of teaching, and judging from their own estimates which are, of course, only rough at best their educational endeavor has, either thru themselves personally or thru their pupils who have become teachers, touched nearly a hundred thousand lives. For the most part these lives have been those of Negroes, altho there is at least one notable instance of a colored graduate conducting a school for whites and several instances where some whites have been taught by persons of color. The grade of teaching done has varied from primary to collegiate. At present three of the alumnæ are teaching in the grades of Kansas City and Buxton; while of the alumni one has recently established a small industrial institute in Mississippi, another has been for five years professor in the state colored agricultural and normal university at Langston, Oklahoma, one has been for fourteen years principal of the State Normal at Prairie View, Texas, and two are trained agriculturalists, directing that line at Tuskegee and Clark University.

The Work of Lawyers

Of the nine who have completed courses in law seven seem to have undertaken the practice of that profession. Of this latter number two failed to respond to the questionnaire; one reports that after eight years' practice in Des Moines and St. Joseph he has gone into the messenger delivery business; another after four years' practice in Des Moines entered the consular service; a fifth, a young attorney in St. Joseph, reports that his cases are mostly criminal and chiefly colored; the sixth, located in Des Moines, combines law with journalism, and says fully one-half his practice consists of white cases; and the seventh, the only one with a solid collegiate training as a basis for legal studies, after nine years' experience, reports a practice of $1,500 to $2,000, largely criminal but including several civil rights cases; he has some white clients, has practiced in state and federal courts in three states and has usually been successful.

Work of Physicians

Of the three physicians in the list two completed liberal arts courses before entering upon the study of medicine. Two are located in northern states and one in Tennessee. Only one has thus far responded to the questionnaire, but this one is no doubt the most successful of all. He made an enviable record at the State University of Iowa, first in liberal arts and then in medicine; he was the first Negro graduate of the college of medicine in that institution and in the examination by the State Board of Medical Examiners he ranked second in a class of fifty-six. For three years he has been practicing at Buxton, Iowa, his home town, a mining community of some 4,500 inhabitants, mostly colored. He is assistant surgeon for the Northwestern Railway and surgeon for the local mining company. He reports a plentiful and varied practice among both whites and blacks. He has recently been chosen state vice-president of the National Medical Association, consisting of the Negro doctors, dentists and pharmacists of the United States.

Work of Pharmacists

Of the four graduates in pharmacy, all had received high school training before beginning the pharmacy course; one had spent a year at Drake University and two held bachelor's degrees from Fisk University. Two are men and one is a woman. One, a graduate of last year, has not yet begun work as a pharmacist; one is proprietor of a drug store and two are managers of drug companies. All are located in communities having a considerable colored element: one in Oklahoma, one in Mississippi and one at Buxton, Iowa. All, however, report patronage from both races. None of these is a graduate of more than three years' standing, so none has a long business record, but the reports of all are hopeful and reassuring:

"I have met with much success since I have broken the barrier of prejudice againt a woman pharmacist by accuracy, neatness and promptness."

"I have only been in business a few months, yet I get patronage from both races and the white druggists give me many professional courtesies."

"The fact that a number of whites from this place took the board examination in October and all failed, while I passed, gave me a high professional standing."

The Work of Dentists

The only dental graduate and practitioner completed his course one year ago. He has located in St. Joseph, Mo., and reports that he has been very successful thus far and has a number of white patients.

Work of Ministers

Of the three who have gone into the ministry two were born in North Carolina and one in Iowa. Two took their first degree in liberal arts and one in law. All had good records as students. One followed his collegiate course with theological seminary training, another entered the ministry only after seven years' experience as a school principal, the third and youngest became a pastor after several years of small-scale business experience. They are located in three separate states: Iowa, Illinois and Missouri. Each represents a different decade of Negro graduation in Iowa. Two are identified with the A. M. E. Church and one with the M. E. Church. The oldest of the three has won recognition in his profession as shown by the fact of his appointment as district superintendent in the M. E. Church.

Work as Editors

The transition from minister to editor is easy and natural, since the most notable figure in the editorial group is the editor of the A. M. E. Church *Review*, Nashville, Tenn., Mr. H. T. Kealing, the oldest colored alumnus of an Iowa college and an editor and lecturer for fifteen years. The only other journalist in the group is John L. Thompson, editor of the one colored journal in the state of Iowa (*The Iowa State Bystander*) and president of the Western Negro Press Association.

Civil Service

Two of the Iowa Negro alumni have entered the civil service: Alexander Clark, one of the older men, died in Liberia, whither he was sent as United States Minister; H. R. Wright, one of the more recent graduates, has been in the consular service five or six years and is now consul at Puerto Cabello, Venezuela.

Political Activity

Most of the male graduates stated that they vote and that their votes are counted. The only exceptions are those living in Alabama, Mississippi and Georgia; they have either failed to reply to questions relating to voting practice and experience or have stated that they do not vote.

Very few have held public office and none has attained to other than minor elective and appointive positions in the state of Iowa, viz: deputy county treasurer, township clerk, file clerk of the general assembly of the state senate, clerk in the hall of archives, judge of election and candidate for nomination for city councilman Des Moines.

Real Estate Ownership

For the seventeen who stated the assessed value of real estate which they owned the holdings ranged in value from $500 to $10,000, and showed an average of $3,000. This number includes a few of the recent graduates, whose property accumulations were naturally small.

Literary Work

Only two seem to have published books, both on religious and moral themes. A dozen or more have contributed articles to magazines, newspapers and bulletins with a wide range of topics and titles, short stories for children, orations and poems, industrial training, agricultural bulletins, abridgment of rights of Negro citizens, discourses on temperance and other social, moral and religious themes.

Advanced Degrees

At least thirteen have taken more than one degree, the second or third degree being in most cases A. M., in some cases professional and occasionally honorary. At least three others have pursued post-graduate study.

Learned Societies

At least ten belong to learned societies, including Phi Beta Kappa, N. E. A., A. A. A. S., National Medical Association, state teachers' associations, etc.

Group Leadership

Aside from the pursuit of their regular vocations most of these men and women have been more or less active in various lines of social and civic service. Many have engaged in religious activities and some have figured rather prominently as laymen in religious organizations, one as a conference delegate and president of Iowa Sunday-school Institute, another as district superintendent of A. M. E. Sunday-schools, another as director of the boys' department of a local Y. M. C. A. and lecturer on physiology and hygiene, one lady has been prominent as a speaker before religious and educational meetings and active in W. C. T. U. and juvenile improvement work, several have turned their attention to leadership in local religious and moral needs. A number have solicited and raised money for schools in which they were interested. One helped in the settlement of the Alton school fight. A few have addressed themselves to the agricultural and industrial uplift of their people and have conducted farmers' congresses or organized farmers' institutes and otherwise led in instruction in agricultural lines. One was former national legal adviser and is now state president of the Afro-American Council. A few have been identified with local business enterprises, such as banks, drug companies, real estate companies, etc.; and one claims the distinction of starting the movement for a Semi-Centennial of Negro Progress since 1863.

The Future

Nearly all these men and women have come up thru adversity and have triumphed despite the heavy odds against them. All express themselves as hopeful for the future of their people in this country. Their suggestions as to the solution of the problems of their race vary widely and reveal diverse philosophies, but for the most part they vouch for the usefulness of these alumni to the communities of which they form a part and to the race whose leadership they in part provide.

Section 7.   Colored Students and Graduates of the University of Kansas [1] (by Mr. Larry M. Peace)

Thirty-nine years ago, when old North College was the University, among the few lank youths and bronzed haired maidens who came from the prairies of Kansas to begin their college careers with the study of grammar, geography, arithmetic, and the like, there was a single dusky face. The enrollment of the colored people in the University of Kansas

---

[1] Printed in *The Graduate Magazine*, University of Kansas.

began then, in 1870, when just one student, a woman, entered the freshman class of the preparatory department. It was not until 1873, however, that this same woman, upon entering what is now the college of liberal arts and sciences, became also the first colored person to do real university work.

During the years subsequent to 1870, there has been no session of the University which has not been attended by colored students. From 1870 to 1890 the number of such students was small; only one, or occasionally two new ones would come each year. From 1890 to 1909 their enrollment has been from four or five to ten new persons each year, the greater numbers having come within the five years just passed. The University register shows that of the forty-four enrolled for the year 1908-1909, nine are in the school for the first time.

The total registration of colored people in the University has been two hundred and eleven: one hundred and forty-three men and sixty-eight women. The six—all, in fact—who came prior to 1876, were women. Beginning with two men in 1876, by far the majority of those who came later were men.

Excepting two, who registered only in the normal department, the twenty-two colored students who came first to the University began their work in the preparatory department. Only six of these, however, remained long enough to enter the collegiate department, where three of them continued to graduation, receiving the degree of bachelor of arts. To one of these three, as will be seen later, was granted the additional degree of bachelor of didactics, the only normal degree ever granted to a colored person by the University of Kansas.

At some time during the past forty years the University has had colored students in every school and in almost every department. At present the writer does not have in mind any course for which some colored person has not enrolled. Just how many have done some work in the graduate school is uncertain, but there have been several, one of whom—a man—received credit for full work leading to a degree. Counting the students of the preparatory department there have been altogether, in what is now the college of liberal arts and sciences, one hundred and eighteen: fifty-nine men and fifty-nine women. In the school of engineering ten men have studied at least thru the freshman year. Thirty men have studied in the school of law, while only two men and seven women have enrolled in the school of fine arts. In the school of pharmacy twenty-six men and two women have been registered, as compared with a total of sixteen men in the school of medicine.

A glance at the following simple table will show the number of men and women who have been enrolled in the various schools of the University, together with the number of degrees granted to each sex.

It will be noticed that no colored women have ever studied in the schools of medicine, law and engineering, and that no colored person has ever graduated from the schools of medicine and fine arts.   It will also be noticed that very few colored women have enrolled for the professional courses, while in the courses in the college they have kept pace with the men not only in number but also in the quality of their work.

	Enrollment			Degrees granted		
	Total	Men	Women	Total	Men	Women
All schools	211	143	68	60	45	15
The Graduate School	(?)	Several	Several	1	1	.
The School of Liberal Arts and Sciences .	118	59	59	31	16	15
The School of Engineering	10	10	.	2	2	.
The School of Law . .	30	30	.	18	18	.
The School of Fine Arts . .	9	2	7	.	.	.
The School of Pharmacy	28	26	2	8	8	.
The School of Medicine	16	16	.	.	.	.

By far the majority of the colored students who have come to the University did not remain thru the sophomore year.   Three-fourths of the preparatory students left before reaching the freshmen year of the college.   Nearly all of those who passed the sophomore year continued to graduation.   This statement is true only for the college.

To the sixty degrees just listed must be added the degree of bachelor of didactics which, together with the degree of bachelor of arts, was granted in 1885 to one man who then became the first colored graduate of the University of Kansas.   The table shows that no colored women have been enrolled in the schools of engineering, law or medicine, and that only two have been enrolled in the school of pharmacy; neither one of the latter, however, continued to graduation.

Of the thirty-one degrees granted by the college fifteen were received by women, all bachelor of arts degrees.   No other degrees have ever been received from the university by colored women.

During the attendance of such students at the University for forty years the number to graduate at any one time has varied, sometimes one, sometimes two, and at a few commencements there has been none.   The greatest number to graduate at any one time finished in 1901, when eight degrees were granted to colored persons: five by the College, two by the School of Pharmacy and one by the School of Law.   During all these years only one person has appeared for a higher degree, one man having received the degree of master of arts in 1908.

Taking no account of gymnasium work, voice culture, theme writing and hygiene, the following table of subjects will show in detail the num_ ber of men and women enrolled in any subject in the list; the total credits given for that subject, and the number of credits received by men and women respectively, the greatest number of credits received by men and women; and finally, the number of each sex who received three or more credits in any one subject:

SUBJECTS	Enrollment			Credits			Greatest credit		Three or more credits	
	Total	Men	Women	Total	Men	Women	Men	Women	Men	Women
English	28	13	15	130	45	85	10	10	5	13
Mathematics . . .	23	12	11	63	34	29	3	3	6	5
Physical sciences .	41	23	18	57	39	18	8	2	5	
Chemistry . .	22	11	11	37	25	12	4	1	5	
Physics .	3	3	. .	3	3	. .	2	.	.	.
Geology	16	9	7	17	11	6	2	1	.	.
Biological sciences .	38	27	21	89	63	26	15	6	7	.
Zoology	19	12	7	33	26	7	7	1	2	.
Botany . . .	22	11	11	45	30	15	6	2	5	.
Entomology	5	4	1	8	7	1	2	1	.	.
Physiology. .	2	. .	2	3	. .	3	. .	2	.	.
Philosophy	15	8	7	36	18	18	4	7	3	2
History .	24	11	13	77	34	43	10	8	5	6
Economics	3	3	. .	10	10	. .	8	.	1	.
Foreign languages .	71	32	39	220	90	140	25	27	12	22
Latin	16	8	8	47	21	26	7	8	3	3
Greek .	7	3	4	22	13	9	6	4	3	2
German .	26	13	13	98	42	56	8	8	6	11
French	18	6	12	46	10	36	2	5	.	6
Spanish .	4	2	2	7	4	3	2	2	.	.
Astronomy . . .	1	1	. .	1	1	. .	1	.	.	.
Education . .	12	5	7	36	17	19	5	4	3	4
Evolution .	8	5	3	9	5	4	2	1	.	.
Sociology	16	10	6	43	24	19	5	6	4	3

A glance at the table will show that when arranged in the order of their popularity, which is determined by the number of credits given in each case, the subjects stand as follows: foreign languages, first; English, second; biological sciences, third; history, fourth; mathematics, fifth; physical sciences, sixth, and social sciences, seventh. In making the calculations economics and sociology are combined. The two subjects are so closely related that they were not carefully kept separate in the table. A few of the credits, therefore, which are assigned to sociology should be given to economics.

It may be seen from the table that the ratios of the credits received by men in the various subjects, to those received by women, can be expressed as follows: English, 1:1.8; mathematics, 1.1:1; physical sciences, 1.2:1; biological sciences, 2.5:1; philosophy, 1:1; history, 1:1.3; social sciences, 1.4:1; foreign languages, 1:1.5. The women clearly outclassed the men, from the standpoint of credits, in the languages and in history, while the men took the lead in biological, physical and social sciences and in mathematics. Upon the whole, the number of men to have received credits in the various subjects is well balanced by that of women.

Three subjects, astronomy, physics and economics, were taken by men only. No subject, however, was taken by women only. Credits in physiology were not assigned to men in the table because such students took the work in the School of Medicine.

An examination of the grades of all colored students who hold degrees from the College of Liberal Arts and Sciences shows no special fitnesses or abilities peculiar to either men or women. Excellent students, as well as very poor ones, were found among those of both sexes in every course. The grade records show that the men must have taken the sciences and the women the languages for other reasons than special ability along these particular lines of work. Excepting the great disparities in the biological sciences and also the physical sciences the number of individual credits by men and women in any particular subject is almost the same for one sex as it is for the other.

Summing up the grades of all colored people who hold degrees from the college and arranging them in the order, grade I, grade II and grade III, the aggregate of I's, II's and III's, sustain the relation 8:12:4. This is an easy but unsatisfactory way of obtaining a notion of the scholarship as a whole.

To compare their standing with that of the white people who hold degrees from the same school is more difficult and even more unsatisfactory. In fact, there is no method of comparison which would be fair to both.

A preliminary comparison was made by selecting from the entire list of those who hold degrees from the college the names of white men and women equal in number to those colored men and women who hold degrees from the same school. One or two names were selected from nearly every class list, by dropping the pencil point upon it and taking the name nearest the point. Thus the records of thirty-one white students, out of a total of seventeen hundred, were secured to be compared with the records made by the thirty-one colored students. Summing up their grades it was found that in the order of grades, I, II and III, as before, they presented the relation 8:9:3—not a great deal different from the 8:12:4 upon the part of the colored students.

In the list of white students was one man who made a complete record of grades one. This standard was not quite reached by any colored student. A few, however, came very near to it, one reaching a total of thirty-two grades one out of thirty-eight credits. Upon the other hand, no individual colored student received quite as many grades three as did an individual white student.

It has already been pointed out that the total number of colored people to attend the University is two hundred and eleven. The total number of white people is said to have been nearly twenty-five thousand. The ratio of the attendance of colored students to that of white students is accordingly about 1:123. The ratio of the number of colored students to finish to the total number to enter is 1:3. The ratio of the number of white students to finish to the number to enter is 1:7.3. The ratio of the number of colored students to graduate to the number of white students to finish is 1:56. An interesting fact to be noticed here is that while there has been one colored student among every one hundred and twenty-three to enter the University there has been an average of one in every fifty-six to finish.

Something of interest pertaining to the colored student in the College of Liberal Arts and Sciences may be gleaned from what has already been said but not a great deal has been said concerning him in the other schools of the University.

The School of Engineering, with only two colored graduates, and the School of Medicine, with none, will be passed without further comment. The School of Law, in the matter of degrees granted, ranks next to the college but owing to the manner of keeping the records no exact data could be obtained. Like the college, however, it has sent out a few excellent students along with the poor ones.

It has been only within the past ten years that any number of colored students have undertaken work in the School of Pharmacy. A few of these have done creditable work.

Whatever have been the accomplishments of the colored student in the class-room, he has taken an insignificant part in university affairs in general. A few have been identified with the various university literary societies, and have even represented the university in debate. This literary inactivity is only a seeming one, for the colored students have done quite creditable things in the town literary societies which they have always maintained. They have generally supported two or three of such societies, holding weekly meetings where all the various literary programs could be rendered. They have maintained exclusive clubs for both men and won,en, one of the most progressive of which is a girls' club of some years' standing. This one is strictly a university girls' club, in which, to quote from their current year book, such subjects as "Macaulay as a Critic," "Religious Troubles in England" and "Warren Hastings" are discussed.

Like their literary powers, the religious talents of the colored students have been little exercised on Mount Oread. Upon the other hand, these same students have taken the lead in the down-town churches. In times past the Sunday-school, the Christian Endeavor, the Baptist Young People's Union and various other church societies would have suffered without their help. They have held all church offices, from Sunday-school teacher and chorister to minister.

While the colored students do not take any part in the social life of the University, in conjunction with the town people they provide themselves with all the latest fads and luxuries of social enjoyment. They have their receptions, their banquets, their club dances, and their annual spring parties.

Tho they have looked well to their literary, religious and social training, they have had very little to do with athletics. Aside from one or two baseball men and a football player the colored students have had very little interest in university sports. This athletic inactivity is due in part to the circumstances under which nearly every one of these students must acquire his education. Aside from the disparity of their numbers it may be found that one of the great differences between white and colored students in the University lies in the circumstances under which each race accomplishes what it does.

If it is more difficult for some colored students to rank high in scholarship from a standpoint of grades than it is for white students it may be owing to the fact that this excellence is not expected of them.   Good work on the part of a colored student nearly always calls forth comment or even expressions of surprise.   The white students do not necessarily have to meet a condition of this nature.

For reasons too obvious to be discussed the associates of the colored student are not men and women schooled and highly cultured, both at home and abroad.   He has not the lure of the Phi Beta Kappa or other honorary society, with friends and relatives to assist him, to advise and direct him, as well as to scheme for him, in order that he may make an enviable record.   The white student may have all of these favors.

Again, nearly all of the colored students are wholly or in part self-supporting.   This was the case with fifty-three out of the sixty who now hold degrees from the University.   It may be that the earning of one's way through school does not need to be a handicap.   Those reporting upon the subject differ in opinion.   Indeed an examination of the records of the colored students shows that the students who labored most strenuously to meet expenses while in school often far surpassed the students who were not at all self-supporting.

It may be, however, that the colored student is somewhat handicapped because of the nature of the work which he must perform for a living. He is usually able to obtain an abundance of work and is willing to do it, but the work is, as a rule, not very remunerative and often takes his time inopportunely.   There were no clerks, stenographers, bookkeepers, and the like, among those fifty-three people who worked their way through the University.   They were table-waiters, janitors, porters, farmers, maids and laundresses.

In addition to these employments they were bound to their social duties.   The white student can forego any social demands with impunity and applause while he is at school.   This is not true of the colored student; his social opportunities and obligations increase with his schooling.   If he is not brave enough to ignore adverse criticism and remain loyal to his studies his scholarship must suffer.   It is true he is needed in society; he is from the best of homes, perhaps, so that much is expected of him; nevertheless, he has yet to learn that toil for a living, society and scholarship do not make an harmonious trio.   Twenty-five of the graduates have been happily married.   Of this number only one couple have been united as the result of a college romance.

Again, it is more difficult for the colored student to succeed because of his home life.   In most cases he comes from parents whose opportunities have not fitted them for assisting him in an educational way.   Often they are innocently indifferent, unsympathetic, and in some cases, even antagonistic.

However well or ill those two hundred former students and graduates fared while in school all are emphatic in their loyalty to a great university where men and women from the humblest walks of life and without money can tarry and get wisdom.

So far as is known all but fourteen of these former students and graduates are still living and doing well. The dead are eleven women and three men. Of these, three—one woman and two men—were graduates. Of the former students eight are practicing physicians, holding degrees from other universities. Three of those holding degrees from the University of Kansas are now studying in other universities for higher degrees. Of the remaining graduates of the University, one, having obtained his degree of doctor of medicine from another school, is practicing medicine; three bachelors of law and twenty-one bachelors of arts are teaching. Of the latter, three are college professors, two are high school teachers and three are ward principals. Two bachelors of art are foreign missionaries. With one exception those holding degrees from the School of Pharmacy are practicing their profession. One law graduate is a minister of the gospel, while another is in the diplomatic service of the United States. Eleven bachelors of law and one bachelor of arts are practicing law. One bachelor of arts and a pharmacist are in the civil service department of the United States. One former student is a successful manufacturer.

Communications from nearly all of these graduates insist that a college training is worth while.

Section 8.   Attitude Toward Negro Students at Oberlin

Oberlin College is especially notable because it was the great pioneer in the work of blotting out the color-line in colleges. During the early thirties Lane Seminary in Cincinnati became a center of anti-slavery enthusiasm. The trustees of the seminary attempted to prohibit the discussion of the slavery question in the institution and this led to a great secession of students. Many of the seceders proposed to go to Oberlin College which had been established in 1833 and there form a theological department, on condition, however, that they have Charles G. Finney, the noted revivalist, as their teacher. Mr. Finney says:

"I had understood that the trustees of Lane Seminary had acted 'over the heads' of the faculty; and, in absence of several of them, had passed the obnoxious resolution that had caused the students to leave. I said, therefore,   that I would not go at any rate, unless two points were conceded by the trustees.   One was, that they should never interfere with the internal regulation of the school but should leave that entirely to the discretion of the faculty.   The other was, that we should be allowed to receive colored people on the same conditions that we did white people; that there should be no discrimination made on account of color.''[1]

These conditions were met, Finney entered upon his work in Oberlin, and the college thus became an anti-slavery stronghold.   Each year since that time has found a considerable number of Negro students enrolled in Oberlin College; and the institution has graduated more Negroes than any other institution of its kind.   There have been the following Negro graduates from Oberlin:

NEGRO GRADUATES FROM OBERLIN

		Living		Dead		Total
		Male	Female	Male	Female	
1844–49..	.	2	. .	2	. .	4
1850–54..	.	. .	. .	1	3	4
1855–59..	.	2	1	1	3	7
1860–64...	.	2	3	2	3	10
1865–69..	.	.	3	6	. .	9
1870–74..	.	1	3	2	2	8
1875–79..	.	3	5	2	.	10
1880–84..	.	7	5	1	. .	13
1885–89..	.	5	4	1	1	11
1890–94..	.	10	9	2	3	24
1895–99..	.	7	1	.	.	8
1900–04..	.	10	6	. .	.	16
1905–09......	.	13	11	1	. . .	25
Total .	.	62	51	21	15	149

Lately the color line has appeared at Oberlin, as the following quotations show:[2]

''   . Like any other condition which depends upon the undergraduate state of mind it changes with the changing classes.   Under normal conditions the attitude of the senior class determines the attitude of the student body and there is some reason to think that the feeling against having colored men in the literary societies is stronger in the present senior class than in the other classes.   If the present attitude were merely sporadic—a temporary aberration of 'the men of 1910—it would not be

[1] Memoirs of Rev. Charles G. Finney, written by himself, p. 333. New York, 1876.
[2] From the *Oberlin Alumni Magazine.*

worth comment. That this is not the case is clear from several facts. In 1905 Alpha Zeta refused to admit a man because of his color. (This action was reversed under pressure from alumni of Alpha Zeta.) Since the graduation of this man no colored men have been members of the literary societies.

"This feeling against the colored men is, of course, not shared by all of the men of the college and we are glad to print here articles from the undergraduates expressing their beliefs on both sides of the question."

" . Phi Delta is not a reformers' club; it is an association of men for literary and social purposes. I know that to me one of the most treasured factors of my society life has been the fellowship and good feeling so evident all thru our work, the feeling of friendship and brotherliness for every fellow member. And this element has had its very important influence on the grade of our literary work, first for Alma Mater, next for the honor of Phi Delta. And, to speak plainly, the presence of a colored man in our ranks would for many of us spoil utterly the social side of society life. It may be a sign of narrowness, but many of us have a very strong feeling in that respect and knew that this step would be a cruel blow at Phi Delta.

"As for the man himself this same feeling would have injured him. Personally, I have nothing but respect and good will toward this individual nor had any of us, but few of us would have been able to give him the glad hand of fellowship and the social equality which would have been his due if admitted. Furthermore, even if he had been taken in and made one of us in every way, many of you older men know full well how small a degree of any such treatment he could have outside Oberlin walls. Would you tantalize a human soul with the vision of a promised land from which an impassable gulf will soon shut him off? And, inasmuch as there are few, if any others of his race, worthy of admission to Phi Delta this step would have isolated him from those with whom his future must be linked."

" For what greater opportunity could come to a society organized to orate and debate on current problems than actually to help solve one of these problems? And how can this particular problem be solved except by the co-operation of the better classes of each race and the encouragement on the part of the dominant race of those who are struggling to overcome the handicap given them by fortune?

"It is hard, of course; for race prejudice is no thing of the imagination, but is real and deeply rooted. But merely because it is hard is no reason why we should shrink from it, but is all the more reason for facing the matter squarely whenever the opportunity is presented. To face the matter squarely is not to hope for some act of congress or other miracle but to make the problem a personal one, for each individual to use his education to supplant prejudice with reason. For race prejudice is directly opposed to reason in that it regards each member of the race as a type rather than as a person. And if college men have not the foresight to look at the situation in its entirety and the justice to judge a college man on his own manly qualities rather than on the traditional qualities of his race, then these men need not be horrified at the cruelties which the same prejudice may lead mobs of their ignorant brothers to perform.''

"In your March issue (p. 224) you announce 'that it has become generally understood' that men like Frederick Douglass, Paul Lawrence Dunbar and Booker Washington 'are not wanted' in the literary societies of the progressive Oberlin of today.

"Is this a fair representation of the 'modern scholarship' of Oberlin, or is it a slanderous fiction? Has color and not character or talent become the 'open sesame' to literary honory on the campus once graced by Tappan Hall, and once the inspiring center of impulse to heroisms of self-sacrifice for men of every color and clime? Has the Missionary Arch, the memorial of men and women who lived and died for those of an off color, crumbled into dust and been forgotten, or has the spirit of some Legree been permitted to come back from the realm of Pluto to misrepresent the Oberlin of today?''

"   I hardly know which surprises me most; the existence of the state of feeling here recorded, or the matter-of-fact way in which the article seems to accept it as something in the order of natural development and progress. Can it be that the present generation of students and instructors have cut themselves loose from the past history and traditions of Oberlin so that they do not realize the foundations on which its present prosperity rests? Oberlin during its early history stood out from other colleges for two fundamental principles, the higher education of women and the brotherhood of man, including the black man. These two ideas gave her friends and prestige in every state of the union and in many foreign countries. It is because of these that Oberlin has a national reputation instead of being a small, local Ohio college. Its liberal and progressive policy has attracted students, friends and money, and so has made its present success possible.''

"   I belonged to Phi Delta in the years 1875 to 1878. If I remember correctly every man in college except three or four belonged to a society, and some colored men were the strongest members. It was not the custom to solicit members for one society rather than another, but new students were expected to visit society meetings and to make their own choice. I never knew of any one being rejected. Any man whose character and scholarship enabled him to stay at Oberlin College could be sure of admission to the society of his own choice. The democratic spirit of all the societies was unquestioned. .

"If it is true that colored young men who desire to join a college society refrain from applying because they fear they will not be welcome, this is a serious misfortune for them, and still more serious for the societies if such an unwillingness to admit them really exists. I can appreciate the sensitive and gentlemanly attitude of those who quietly hold back from going where they suspect they may not be wanted, but I am alarmed for those who are willing to have any share in barring out any of their fellow students from the valuable opportunities of our Oberlin College societies.''

Section 9.   The Number of Negro College Graduates

The number so far as can be ascertained of persons of Negro descent who have been graduated from American colleges may be arranged in the following tables:

NEGRO COLLEGE GRADUATES BY YEARS

1823 .	. 1	1861 .	3	1879 .	48	1895 .	. 130
1826 .	. 1	1862 .	3	1880 .	50	1896 .	. 104
1828 .	. 1	1864 .	2	1881 .	55	1897 .	. 128
1841 .	. 1	1865 .	6	1882 .	39	1898 .	. 144
1844 .	. 2	1867 .	4	1883 .	74	1899 .	89
1847 .	. 1	1868 .	9	1884 .	64	1900 .	92
1849 .	. 3	1869 .	. 11	1885 .	. 100	1901 .	. 145
1850 .	. 1	1870 .	. 26	1886 .	94	1902 .	. 128
1851 .	. 1	1871 .	. 15	1887 .	90	1903 .	. 148
1852 .	. 1	1872 .	. 26	1888 .	87	1904 .	. 139
1853 .	. 1	1873 .	. 29	1889 .	85	1905 .	. 267
1854 .	. 1	1874 .	. 27	1890 .	95	1906 .	. 182
1856 .	. 5	1875 .	. 25	1891 .	99	1907 .	. 133
1858 .	. 1	1876 .	. 37	1892 .	70	1908 .	. 224
1859 .	. 1	1877 .	. 43	1893 .	. 137	1909 .	. 155
1860 .	. 6	1878 .	. 37	1894 .	. 130		
						Total .	. 3,856

The following table shows the increase by decades from three graduates during the decade 1820-1829 to 1,613 graduates during the decade 1900-1909:

Decade	Number of Negro college graduates
1820–1829 .	3
1830–1839 .	. . .
1840–1849 .	7
1850–1859	12
1860–1869	44
1870–1879	313
1880–1889	738
1890–1899	1,126
1900–1909 .	1,613
Total .	3,856

NEGRO GRADUATES OF OTHER COLLEGES (BY SEX)

INSTITUTION	Male	Female	Total	INSTITUTION	Male	Female	Total
Oberlin	83	66	149	University of Illinois	7	.	7
Dartmouth	14	.	14	University of Wooster	1	.	1
Ohio State	9	.	13	University of Vermont	3	.	3
Radcliffe	.	4	4	Middlebury	3	1	4
Smith	.	4	4	Southwest Kansas	1	.	1
Iowa State	2	.	2	St. Stephens	4	.	4
Vassar	.	1	1	Trinity	1	.	1
Western Reserve	9	4	13	Otterbein	1	1	2
Indiana	8	.	8	Tabor	3	.	3
University of Pittsburg	10	.	10	Moravian	1	.	1
College of the City of N.Y.	2	.	2	Mt. Union	1	.	1
University of Minnesota	8	.	8	Ohio Wesleyan	2	1	3
Harvard	41	.	41	Marietta	6	.	6
Yale	37	.	37	McKendree	.	1	1
Columbia	3	.	3	Ohio	3	.	3
Univ. of Pennsylvania	29	.	29	Denison	6	1	7
Amherst	14	.	14	University of Rochester	1	.	1
University of California	2	1	3	Purdue	3	.	3
Northwestern	4	1	5	Pomona	1	.	1
Boston	3	.	3	Wesleyan (Conn.)	5	.	5
Coe	2	.	2	Bloomington	.	1	1
Iowa Wesleyan	5	.	5	Iowa State College	2	.	2
Bowdoin	1	.	1	Lafayette	1	.	1
Butler	3	1	4	Albion	3	.	3
Case	2	.	2	Amity	.	1	1
Catholic	2	.	2	Franklin	3	.	3
Cornell College	1	.	1	Bates	12	1	13
Dickinson	1	.	1	Rutgers	1	.	1
Beloit	2	1	3	Westminster	2	.	2
Bucknell	7	.	7	Eureka	1	.	1
Rhode Island State	1	.	1	Hiawatha	1	.	1
Baldwin	2	.	2	Hiram	3	.	3
Washington and Jefferson	2	1	3	Heidleburg	1	.	1
Hillsdale	3	.	3	Lawrence	.	1	1
Monmouth	1	.	1	Lebanon	2	.	2
University of Cincinnati	1	2	3	Wittenburg	2	2	4
Kansas	4	2	6	Lombard	1	.	1
Armour	5	.	5	Univ. of Washington	1	.	1
University of Nebraska	5	1	6	Univ. of So. California	1	.	1
New York	3	.	3	Lake Forest	1	.	1
Illinois	1	.	1	Grove City	1	.	1
Mt. Holyoke	.	2	2	Geneva	7	3	10
Shurtliff	2	.	2	Syracuse	2	.	2
Bellevue	1	.	1	Berea	31	4	35
Adrian	1	1	2	New Hampshire	1	.	1
Allegheny	1	.	1	University of Kansas	45	15	60
Colby	3	.	3	Wheaton	2	1	3
De Pauw	1	.	1	Wellesley	.	3	3
Penn	.	1	1	Williams	7	.	7
Olivet	1	1	2	University of Denver	3	1	4
Washburn	4	3	7	Grinnell	1	.	1
Omaha	1	.	1	Hamilton	1	.	1
University Park	3	1	4	Cornell University	7	3	10
Upper Iowa	.	1	1	Total	549	144	693

The above table is made from the reports of 107 colleges (not Negro) and shows the total number of Negro graduates to be 693; 549 or 79.2 per cent of them are men while 144 or 20.8 per cent are women.

GRADUATES OF NEGRO COLLEGES (BY SEX)

INSTITUTION	Male	Fe-male	Total	INSTITUTION	Male	Fe-male	Total
New Orleans	36	14	50	Wilberforce ..	114	24	138
Branch . . .	10	2	12	Bennett . . .	68	71	139
Georgia State ..	4	. . .	4	Geo. R. Smith .	6	. . .	· 6
Paul Quinn .	37	18	55	Spelman. . . .	. . .	13	13
Bishop	28	2	30	Atlanta Baptist ..	42	. . .	42
Wiley .	35	5	40	Benedict	22	4	26
Clark . .	57	36	93	Tougaloo	9	3	12
Knoxville .	54	18	72	Paine .	15	4	19
Howard . .	159	23	182	Shaw .	136	82	218
Tillotson.	1	. . .	1	Walden .	62	15	77
Hartshorn Memorial..	. . .	2	2	Straight	28	9	37
Morris Brown ..	27	3	30	Virginia Union	46	. . .	46
Shorter .	18	14	32	Colored A. & M. (Okla.) ..	2	1	3
Claflin ..	61	18	79	St. Augustine ..	42	15	57
Atlanta .	129	34	163	Arkansas Baptist ..	11	4	15
Biddle ..	275	. . .	275	Central City .	3	. . .	3
Fisk ..	187	58	245				
Lincoln .	617	. .	617	Total	2450	514	2964

The above table is made from the reports of 34 Negro colleges and shows a total of 2,964 graduates; 2,450 or 82.7 per cent of them are men, while 514 or 17.3 per cent of them are women.   Most, tho not all, of these schools are co-educational.   Biddle, Lincoln, Atlanta Baptist College and Virginia Union University are schools for male students, while Spelman and Hartshorn Memorial are for female students only.

It is shown that the following Negro colleges have sent forth a hundred or more graduates:

Atlanta University   . 163
Bennett College .   .   . ✦.   139
Biddle University .   .   . 275
Fisk University .   . 245
Howard University   .   . 182
Lincoln University   . .   . 617
Shaw University   .   .   . 218
Wilberforce University   . 138

NEGRO GRADUATES OF OTHER COLLEGES BY TIME GROUPS

NAME OF COLLEGE	1820-1829	1830-1839	1840-1849	1850-1854	1855-1859	1860-1864	1865-1869	1870-1874	1875-1879	1880-1884	1885-1889	1890-1894	1895-1899	1900-1904	1905-1909	Class not given	Total
Oberlin			4	4	7	10	9	8	10	13	11	24	8	16	25		149
Dartmouth							1	1	1	1			3	2	5		14
Ohio State												2	4		7		13
Radcliffe													1	1	2		4
Smith														3	1		4
Iowa State												1		1			2
Vassar																1	1
Western Reserve												1	2	4	6		13
Indiana													4	1	3		8
Univ. of Pittsburg												1	2	2	5		10
College City of N.Y.															2		2
Univ. of Minnesota										1	1	2	1	2	1		8
Harvard									1	2	1	3	4	10	20		41
Yale									1	3	1	2	6	9	15		37
Columbia										1		1	1				3
Univ. of Penn.										2	2	9	6	6	4		29
Amherst										1		3	1	3	6		14
Univ. of California															3		3
Northwestern															5		5
Boston													3				3
Coe														1	1		2
Iowa Wesleyan											2	2	1				5
Bowdoin		1															1
Butler												1	1	1		1	4
Case																2	2
Catholic																2	2
Cornell College														1			1
Dickinson														1			1
Beloit												1	1	1			3
Bucknell									1	1	2		2	1			7
Baldwin										1			1				2
Rhode Island State												1					1
Washington & Jeff'n												2		1			3
Hillsdale											1		2				3
Monmouth														1			1
Univ. of Cincinnati													1	1	1		3
Kansas State													1	3	2		6
Armour Institute													2	2	1		5
Univ. of Nebraska													2	1	3		6
New York													1		2		3
Illinois													1				1
Mt. Holyoke											1		1				2
Shurtliffe									1							1	2
Bellevue													1				1
Adrian						1				1							2
Allegheny											1						1
Colby											1	1				1	3
De Pauw												1					1
Penn																1	1
Olivet									1							1	2
Washburn													1	2	3	1	7
Omaha													1				1
University Park													1	2	1		4
Upper Iowa														1			1
University of Illinois														2	5		7
Univ. of Wooster													1				1
Univ. of Vermont																3	3
Middlebury	1		1							1				1			4
Southwest Kansas														1			1
St. Stephens														1		3	4
Trinity																1	1
Otterbein														1		1	2
Tabor																3	3

NEGRO GRADUATES OF OTHER COLLEGES BY TIME GROUPS—CONTINUED

NAME OF COLLEGE	1820-1829	1830-1839	1840-1849	1850-1854	1855-1859	1860-1864	1865-1869	1870-1874	1875-1879	1880-1884	1885-1889	1890-1894	1895-1899	1900-1904	1905-1909	Class not given	Total
Moravian															1		1
Mt. Union																1	1
Ohio Wesleyan															1	2	3
Marietta									1		1	3				1	6
McKendree												1					1
Ohio	1			1												1	3
Denison										1					1	1	3
Univ. of Rochester										1	1	1	1			3	7
Purdue												1					1
Pomona												1		1	1		3
Wesleyan (Conn.)						2										3	5
Bloomington															1		1
Iowa												1		1			2
Lafayette			1														1
Albion																3	3
Amity																1	1
Franklin			1														3
Bates							1	1	1	2	2	5	1				13
Rutgers											1						1
Westminster						1	1										2
Eureka														1			1
Hiawatha											1						1
Hiram							1				1		1				3
Heidleburg																1	1
Laurence																1	1
Lebanon																2	2
Wittenburg													2	1	1		4
Lombard											1						1
Univ. of Washington																1	1
Univ. of So. California																1	1
Lake Forest																1	1
Grove City																1	1
Geneva							1	2	2	2	1					2	10
Syracuse																2	2
Berea																35	35
New Hampshire											1						1
Univ. of Kansas																60	60
Wheaton																3	3
Wellesley														1		2	3
Williams											1	2	1	1		2	7
Univ. of Denver												1	2		1		4
Grinnell														1			1
Hamilton												1					1
Cornell University																10	10
Total	3		7	5	7	12	13	15	19	33	36	78	81	89	149	146	693

GRADUATES OF NEGRO

NAME OF COLLEGE	Before 1876	1876	1877	1878	1879	1880	1881	1882	1883	1884	1885	1886	1887	1888	1889	1890
New Orleans					3		2		2		2				1	2
Branch Normal								1	1	4	2					1
Georgia State																
Paul Quinn															2	
Bishop										1		1				1
Wiley														1		
Clark									1	1	2	3	3	1	4	
Knoxville									2	1	1		1	5	5	3
Howard	5	2	2	1	2	4	6			4	2	3	3	2	6	4
Tillotson																
Hartshorn Memorial																
Morris Brown																
Shorter																
Claflin																
Atlanta		6	3	4	5	5	5	2	3	3	2	4	4		3	3
Biddle		1	4	2	4	2	6	3	1	3	6	7	3	3	3	2
Fisk	4			2	2	4	6	5	1	7	4	13	3	8	12	12
Lincoln	48	8	6	6	4	6	5	8	17	14	23	23	20	19	17	6
Wilberforce	11	1	1	2	1	3	4	1	3	5	2	5	3	4	7	1
Bennett																
George R. Smith																
Spelman																
Atlanta Baptist																
Benedict																1
Tougaloo																
Paine																
Shaw					6	5	12	5	4	6	4	10	12	4	13	19
Walden					1		5	5	1						3	3
Straight		2	1	3	8		5		5		5	1		2		
Virginia Union																
Colored A. and M. (Okla.)																
St. Augustine												11				
Arkansas Baptist																
Central City																
Total	68	20	19	30	33	43	50	23	50	45	69	75	53	62	69	54

It is impossible to ascertain the exact number of Negroes who have graduated from colleges in the North for many of these institutions keep no record of race or nationality of their graduates. We quote from the replies from Brown University and from the University of Michigan which are typical of such cases:

University of Michigan.—"I find that in our alumni records no mention is made as to the color of graduates."

Brown University.—"There is no one who can give a list of the Negro graduates of Brown University. We have never kept any list of students according to race or nationality. While from one point of view

COLLEGES BY YEARS

	1891	1892	1893	1894	1895	1896	1897	1898	1899	1900	1901	1902	1903	1904	1905	1906	1907	1908	1909	Class not given	Total
	4			1	2	1	1	2	1	2	5	2	3	5	1	2	2	1	1	2	50
		1			1				1				2								12
									1	1		2									4
	4		1	1	3	1	2	4	2	1	1	4	7	3	4	2	7	5			55
	1		1		1			1	2		2	1		3	4	6	13				30
	1	1	1				1	2		2	4	1	3	4	4	3	7	3			40
	1	3		2			2			3	2	2	4	6	8	8	8	9	5	15	93
	1		2	3	1	2	3	8	2	1	5	4		8	8	4	3	4	2		72
	2	2	5	5	3	3	2	8	5	4	11	7	7	6	11	10	6	17	17		182
																			1		1
									2												2
									2	3	2	3	3	1		8	1	3	2	2	30
																				32	32
																				79	79
	5		2	7	4	5	4	3	9	4	6	4	10	6	8	7	10	10	7		163
	7	7	9	10	12	9	6	8	10	15	13	13	14	14	21	22	13	13	11		275
	12	6	14	8	11	15	9	11	11	8	13	9	22	21	22	23	16	20	34		376
	19	18	20	36	27	19	19	18	21	26	27	23	27	28	18	24	19				617
	1	2	2	4	2	5	6	6	8	6	3	5	2		10	8	7	9			138
	2	2	4	5	8	3	14	15		15	8	8		2	7	11	5	4	10		139
																				6	6
								3	3			2		4			1	1	3	2	13
		2			1						3	2	1		2	7	5	1	3	2	42
				1						1	1	1	3	1	3	6	1	1	3		26
		1									1	2	3	2			1				12
			3	2	3	2				1	2	3	2								19
		6	18	10	9	5	6	3		5	3	10	3	5	1	7	6	4	17		218
	4				1	2	4	2	10	2	4		3	2	2	3	1		4	8	77
	1					1				2	3		1			1		1			37
												4	7	4	5	3	9	6	5		46
												3						8			3
	2	2	1	1			2	2	1	2	3	2	3	2	1	6	4	5	7		57
										3								4	2	1	3	15
																				3	3
	64	**54**	**83**	**99**	**88**	**76**	**85**	**107**	**93**	**105**	**122**	**116**	**129**	**127**	**158**	**160**	**150**	**137**	**128**	**120**	**2,964**

such distinctions are valuable, from another point of view it may be said that the constant effort of the college should be to ignore such distinctions, and replace them with the distinctions of ability and character. It is possibly for this reason that we have never kept any record of race distinctions among our alumni."

It is similarly true of other schools, which consequently do not appear in the above tables, tho they are known to have graduated Negroes. The University of Chicago, Columbia University and Tufts College are but a few additions to this list—all of which have sent forth Negro graduates of power and efficiency. There are also a few notable cases of American Negroes who have been graduated from colleges abroad.

It is probably safe to say that 5,000 Negro Americans have graduated from college.

Section 10.   Statistics of Certain Living Negro Graduates

In answer to the questionnaire sent to Negro college graduates about eight hundred answers were received.   These answers come from graduates of eighty-one colleges as follows:

NEGRO COLLEGES

Allen	Morris Brown
Atlanta Baptist	New Orleans
Atlanta University	Paine
Bennett	St. Augustine
Biddle	Shaw
Bishop	Shorter
Central City	Spelman
Claflin	State (Georgia)
Clark	Straight
Fisk	Talladega
Geo. R. Smith	Tougaloo
Gilbert	Virginia Union
Howard	Walden
Knoxville	Wilberforce
Leland	Wiley
Lincoln	

OTHER COLLEGES

Adelbert	New York University
Albion	Oberlin
Allegheny	Ohio State
Amherst	Olivet
Amity	Otterbein
Armour	Pomona
Bates	Rutgers
Bellevue	Shurtliff
Berea	Stanford
Boston University	Tabor
Brown	University of Cincinnati
Bucknell	University of Denver
Colby	University of Illinois
Cornell	University of Indiana
Dartmouth	University of Iowa
Denison	University of Kansas

Dickinson
Franklin
Harvard
Hillsdale
Kansas State
Lawrence
Massachusetts Agr. Col.
Middlebury
Nebraska State University

University of Minnesota
University of Pennsylvania
University of Rochester
University of Vermont
Washburn
Wesleyan
Western Reserve
Williams
Yale

NEGRO GRADUATES REPORTING, BY COLLEGE AND TIME OF GRADUATION

INSTITUTION	1850-1869	1870-1889	1890-1899	1900-1909	Total
Adelbert				1	1
Albion				2	2
Allegheny		1			1
Allen		1			1
Amherst			1		1
Amity				1	1
Armour				1	1
Atlanta Baptist			5	26	31
Atlanta University		14	12	29	55
Bates				3	3
Bellevue				1	1
Bennett		1	7	11	19
Berea		4	4	2	10
Biddle		13	16	19	48
Bishop		1		2	3
Boston University			1		1
Brown		1	3	2	6
Bucknell			1		1
Central City			1	1	2
Claflin		5	7	12	24
Clark		4	4	5	13
Colby			2		2
Cornell				2	2
Dartmouth				4	4
Dennison			2	2	4
Dickinson				1	1
Fisk		23	36	58	117
Franklin			1	1	2
Geo. R. Smith				3	3
Gilbert				1	1
Harvard	1			3	4
Hillsdale	1				1
Howard		7	4	6	17
Kansas State				1	1
Knoxville		6	9	14	29
Lawrence		1			1
Leland		2	7	8	17
Lincoln	1	21	19	20	61
Massachusetts Ag. Col.				1	1
Middlebury		1			1
Morris Brown			1	6	7
Nebraska State Univ.				1	1
New Orleans			1	3	4
New York University				1	1
Oberlin	3	4	6	13	26
Ohio State	1		3	4	8
Olivet			1		1
Otterbein			1		1
Paine			3	8	11
Pomona				1	1
Rutgers			1		1
St. Augustine		2	2	4	8
Shaw		15	9	15	39
Shorter			1	3	4
Shurtliff				1	1
Spelman				7	7
Stanford			1		1
State (Georgia)			1		1
Straight		1	1	2	4
Tabor		1	1		2
Talladega				13	13
Tougaloo				9	9
Univ. of Cincinnati			1		1
University of Denver		1			1
University of Illinois				4	4
University of Indiana			1	1	2
University of Iowa			1	1	2
University of Kansas		1	3	2	6
Univ. of Minnesota				1	1
Univ. of Pennsylvania			1		1
Univ. of Rochester			1		1
Univ. of Vermont				1	1
Virginia Union				17	17
Walden		2	7	3	12
Washburn				2	2
Wesleyan		2	1	4	7
Western Reserve				1	1
Wilberforce		8	7	7	22
Wiley			2	7	9
Williams			1		1
Yale		1	3	1	5

TABLE SHOWING PLACE OF BIRTH AND PRESENT RESIDENCE OF NEGRO GRADUATES REPORTING

BORN IN (LIVING IN →)	New England States	Southern North Atlantic States	Northern South Atlantic States	Southern South Atlantic States	Eastern North Central States	Western North Central States	Eastern South Central States	Western South Central States	Rocky Mountain States	Basin and Plateau States	Pacific States	Outside United States	Unknown	Total
Louisiana .	1	. .	.	1	1	.	.	4	24	.	.	.	1	32
Kentucky . .	1	. .	.	2	1	5	2	14	1	.	.	.	1	27
Illinois. .	2	. .	.	2	.	3	.	1	1	.	.	.	.	9
Ohio . .	.	1	.	4	14	4	.	2	3	.	.	.	.	32
Tennessee . .	3	2	.	3	4	5	43	6	.	.	.	1	1	68
Virginia	1	6	28	6	5	5	11	3	.	.	.	.	5	70
South Carolina	.	9	7	62	6	1	4	7	.	.	.	1	2	99
North Carolina	.	4	12	86	4	.	.	3	4	.	.	.	2	115
Florida	.	1	1	2	.	.	.	1	2	.	.	.	.	7
Kansas	1	1	.	.	.	.	7	.	.	.	.	.	1	10
Indiana . .	.	.	.	.	3	.	.	.	1	.	.	.	.	4
Mississippi	.	3	2	.	1	.	.	15	7	.	.	.	.	28
Texas . .	.	.	.	.	.	.	1	2	14	.	.	.	.	17
Michigan	.	.	1	.	3	.	.	1	.	.	.	.	.	5
Maryland .	1	2	9	.	3	1	.	.	3	.	.	.	1	20
Missouri . .	.	.	1	2	.	7	1	.	1	.	.	.	2	14
Arkansas .	.	1	1	1	.	1	.	7	.	.	.	.	1	12
Ontario. . .	.	.	.	.	.	1	.	.	.	.	.	.	.	1
Canada . .	.	1	.	1	.	.	1	.	.	.	.	.	.	3
Nova Scotia . .	.	.	.	1	.	.	.	.	.	.	.	.	.	1
South Africa . . .	.	.	.	1	.	.	.	.	.	.	.	.	.	1
British West Indies . .	1	.	.	.	.	.	.	.	.	.	.	.	.	1
Alabama .	6	1	2	8	2	1	20	7	1	.	.	.	.	48
Georgia .	1	2	4	89	4	4	12	6	.	.	1	.	.	123
Iowa.	.	.	.	.	1	4	.	1	.	.	.	.	.	6
Massachusetts	.	1	.	.	.	.	.	1	.	.	.	.	.	2
Connecticut . .	1	.	.	.	.	.	.	.	.	.	.	.	.	1
New Jersey . .	.	1	.	.	1	.	.	.	.	.	.	.	.	2
New York . .	.	.	3	.	.	.	1	.	.	.	.	.	.	4
Pennsylvania .	.	3	1	2	1	1	2	1	.	.	1	.	.	12
West Virginia	.	.	3	.	.	.	1	.	.	.	1	.	.	5
District of Columbia	.	1	8	.	.	2	.	.	.	.	.	.	.	11
West Indies . .	.	.	.	2	.	.	1	.	.	.	.	.	.	3
Rhode Island	.	1	.	.	1	.	.	.	.	.	.	.	.	2
Unknown . .	.	1	.	4	.	.	.	1	.	.	.	.	1	7
Total .	19	42	92	276	61	47	141	99	2	.	3	2	18	802

From the above table the following facts concerning birth-place of these 802 graduates are noted:

*South Atlantic States**

Maryland	20 .	. 2.5 per cent
District of Columbia.	11 .	1.4 " "
Virginia . . .	70 .	. 8.7 " "
West Virginia .	5 .	.62 " "
North Carolina	. 115 . . .	14.3 " "
South Carolina	99	12.3 " "
Georgia .	123 .	15.2 " "
Florida .	7	.87 " "
Total .	450	56.1 per cent

South Central States

Kentucky . .	27	3.3 per cent
Tennessee .	68 .	8.5 " "
Alabama .	48 .	5.9 " "
Mississippi	28 .	3.5 " "
Arkansas	12 .	1.5 " "
Louisiana .	32 .	4. " "
Texas .	17	2.1 " "
Total .	232	28.9 per cent
Total South .	682 .	. 85 " "

The leading states of the North on the basis of birth of Negro college graduates reporting are as follows:

Ohio.. 32 | Missouri . 14 | Pennsylvania . 12 | Kansas . 10 | Illinois . . 9

Further using the census nomenclature we draw the following facts concerning present residence of these 802 graduates:

Present residence	Number	Per cent of total
New England States	19	2.4
Southern North Atlantic States .	42	5.2
Northern South Atlantic States .	92	11.5
Southern South Atlantic States .	276	34.4
Eastern North Central States .	61	7.6
Western North Central States	47	5.9
Eastern South Central States .	141	17.6
Western South Central States	99	12.3
Elsewhere	25	3.1
Total .	802	100

The following table is a clear statement of the movements of these graduates:

---

* Census nomenclature used.

BORN IN	Total	LIVING IN			
		North	South	Places outside U. S.	Unknown
North .	103=100%	65=63 %	35=34 %	1=1 %	2=2 %
South	682=100%	102=15 %	563=82.5%	2= .3%	15=2.2%
Places outside United States .	10=100%.	3=30 %	7=70 %	. . . .	. . . .
Unknown .	7=100%	5=71 %	1=14 %	. . . . .	1=14 %
Total .	802=100%	175=21.8%	606=75.6%	3=3 %	18=2.2%

The above table shows that of 103 graduates born in the North, sixty-five or 63 per cent of them remained in the North, while thirty-five or 34 per cent went to the South to labor among their people. Of 682 graduates born in the South 102 or 15 per cent of them went to the North, while 563 or 82.5 per cent of them remained in the South.

These statistics cover only about one-fourth of the living Negro college graduates but they are typical of the whole group. Three facts are clearly shown:

1. The greater part of the labors of college-bred Negro Americans is expended in the South where the great masses of Negroes dwell.

2. The great majority of southern born Negro college graduates have remained in the South to labor among their people.

3. There has been a continuous stream of northern born college-bred Negroes who have come to the South and joined in the work of lifting black people to higher planes of culture and intelligence.

There has been a rapid and encouraging development in the family life of the American Negro since the emancipation. For more than two hundred years the Negroes in America suffered the social evils of the slave regime. It may be said that the greatest evils of slavery in America were the breaking up of family ties and the consequent premium placed upon promiscuous sexual relations. The evident tendencies then were toward uncertainty of and disregard for the marriage vow. During the forty odd years of freedom great progress has been made in the eradication of these evils as is evidenced by the number of well ordered Negro homes built upon constant family relations. In this great work the college-bred men and women of the Negro race have had a large share.

The statistics are meagre but they show something of present tendencies.

CONJUGAL CONDITION

	Male	Female	Total
Married ..	465=67.3%	34=31.1 %	499= 62 %
Single ..	207=30 %	72=66.05%	279= 35 %
Widowed	17= 2.4%	2= 1.88%	19= 2 %
Divorced	1	1	2
Total	690=100 %	109=100 %	799=100 %

The above table shows that 67.3 per cent of the males and 31.1 per cent of the females reporting are married. It must be remembered that many of these reports come from graduates of quite recent years. The per cent of divorced is exceedingly low.

AGE AT MARRIAGE

AGE AT MARRIAGE	Males	Females	Total
Under 20 years	3	. .	3
20-24 years	49	10	59
25-29 years	170	17	187
30-34 years	151	3	154
35-39 years	53	. .	53
40-44 years	19	. .	19
45 years and over .	9	1	10
Not given .	11	3	14
Total	465	34	499

The above table shows that of the 465 male graduates reporting themselves as married the majority have married between the ages of twenty-five and thirty-four, and of the thirty-four female graduates reporting themselves as married the majority have married between the ages of twenty and twenty-nine.

The tables which follow contain statistics of children born to families of Negro college graduates reporting themselves as having been married. The first of these tables shows that the families of 134 male graduates and of seven female graduates are childless. Here also it must be remembered that not a few of these reports come from graduates of quite recent date. The families of the remaining graduates reporting themselves as having been married report from one child to fourteen children each; that is, the families of 378 graduates report 1,411 children or roughly speaking an average of four children per family. The average for all families of graduates reporting themselves as having been married would be slightly less.

The following table shows:

CHILDREN BORN TO FAMILIES OF GRADUATES REPORTING

CHILDREN	Number Families of		CHILDREN	Number Families of	
	Male graduates	Female graduates		Male graduates	Female graduates
No children .	134	7	Eight children .	9	
One child . .	82	7	Nine children	10	
Two children .	55	4	Ten children . .	6	
Three children	63	4	Eleven children	2	1
Four children .	44	.	Twelve children	3	1
Five children	36	3	Thirteen children	2	
Six children . .	24	2	Fourteen children	1	
Seven children	17	2			

The following tables combine the number of children born to and the number of children lost by families of Negro graduates reporting. The death statistics include still-birth. It is seen that the families of 208 graduates reporting children have lost none. The remaining 170 families report the loss of one child to eight children each; that is, a total loss of 344 children or an average loss of barely one child per family of the families reporting children.

It is no small part of the mission of the educated to see to it that children are well born. The college-bred Negro American has helped in this direction. Meagre as these statistics are they are nevertheless of value.

FAMILIES OF MALE GRADUATES REPORTING

FAMILIES HAVING BORN / FAMILIES LOSING BY DEATH (INCLUDING STILL-BIRTH)	One child	CHILDREN													Total
		2	3	4	5	6	7	8	9	10	11	12	13	14	
	82	55	63	44	36	24	17	9	10	6	2	3	2	1	354
No children .	68	41	39	23	11	6	2	3	3	..	..	..	..	..	196
One child ..	14	10	15	12	6	4	5	1	4	..	..	..	..	..	71
Two children .	..	4	7	5	12	8	5	2	1	3	1	..	1	..	49
Three children	..	..	2	3	4	4	2	1	1	..	1	..	..	..	18
Four children .	..	..	..	1	2	2	2	..	..	1	..	1	..	..	9
Five children .	..	..	..	..	1	..	..	1	1	2	..	..	..	1	6
Six children ..	..	..	..	..	..	..	1	1	..	..	..	2	..	..	4
Seven children	..	..	..	..	..	..	..	..	..	..	..	..	..	..	.
Eight children..	..	..	..	..	..	..	..	..	..	..	..	..	1	..	1
Total .	82	55	63	44	36	24	17	9	10	6	2	3	2	1	354

FAMILIES OF FEMALE GRADUATES REPORTING

FAMILIES HAVING BORN / FAMILIES LOSING BY DEATH (INCLUDING STILL-BIRTH)	One child	CHILDREN											Total
		2	3	4	5	6	7	8	9	10	11	12	
	7	4	4	..	3	2	2	..	..	..	1	1	24
No children ..	6	2	1	..	3	..	..	..	..	..	..	..	12
One child ..	1	..	3	..	..	..	1	..	..	..	..	..	5
Two children .	..	2	..	..	..	1	1	..	..	..	..	..	4
Three children	..	..	..	..	..	1	..	..	..	..	1	..	2
Four children .	..	..	..	..	..	..	..	..	..	..	..	1	1
Total .	7	4	4	..	3	2	2	..	..	..	1	1	24

Section 11.   Early Life and Training

Reports of early life and training do not lend themselves to ready tabulation.   The following quotations are taken from the reports of these Negro college graduates and are both typical and interesting—showing as they do something of the childhood and youth thru which these men and women have passed.

Men

"I was carefully reared by parents who had been slaves, attended public schools, removed to Ohio and attended high school."

"I was born and reared on a cotton farm.   My early training was such as could be received in an ex-slave home and three-months-in-the-year school.   Mother and father were honest tho unlettered and strove to make the best of their opportunities and left that impression upon their children.   Best of all, I was reared in a Christian home."

"I went from Virginia to Vermont December 23, 1863. I worked on the farm nine months during the year and attended common school three months. I did this till 1872. I then went to Andover, Massachusetts, March 7, 1872. Attended Phillips Andover Academy from 1872 to 1875; then to Middlebury College, Vermont, 1875 to 1880; Boston University, 1880 to 1883."

"My early life was spent on the farm. My early training was two months of public school each year and studying at night by lightwood knots. I went from this to the graded school of Wilson, North Carolina, and from there to Lincoln University, Pennsylvania."

"I was born of poor, hard-working parents and was left an orphan at eleven years. I went to night school in the town where I was being reared by a family of white people who were the ex-owners of my parents. I entered school as a day student at age of seventeen, completed the academic course at twenty and then went to college."

"Being born a slave, my early training was quite meagre until I was eleven or twelve years old, having simply learned to read and spell well up to my twelfth year. My literary training was obtained in Tennessee, to which I was brought in very early life."

"My early life was one of poverty and longing for better things."

"I was born on a farm and remained there until I was well up in age. I have chopped cotton, worked corn, pulled hay, because I had no scythe to cut it, peddled wood at the Fayetteville, North Carolina, market many a winter with no shoes on and clothing extremely scarce.   My life was one of struggle from the time I could remember but in the future I saw a star of hope and pushed in that direction every time I saw an opportunity to advance. I went to a country school in a log house in Cumberland county, North Carolina. I went to Wilmington to live and there went to night school four or five months."

"My father deserted home when I was about five years old. My mother died when I was twelve years old, leaving me in the care of an illiterate foster mother. She was very kind to me and did laundry work that I might be allowed to attend school. I finished the public school course in 1895. In the summer of 1896 I went to Rhode Island to work. From that time until I finished school in 1905 I paid my own expenses by doing hotel work in summer."

"I was born a slave. I learned the alphabet in 1868 near Nashville, Tennessee, and graduated from college in 1878."

"Early life on a plantation amid surroundings incident to slave life. Attended public school more or less irregularly."

"I was a slave until eleven years of age. I learned the bricklayer's trade. I entered college in 1875."

"I was born in the country, worked on farm till eighteen years old, then worked for railroad three years. I went to school about four months before I was twenty."

"I passed my early life on the farm near the town of Franklinton, North Carolina, and was trained in the Christian Institute and Albion Academy. I never had the support of a father but was obedient to the direction of a loving mother to whom I owe all I am and all I hope to be."

"I worked on a farm and attended rural schools until I was sixteen and then entered Fisk University."

"I was born a slave and was freed by the Emancipation Proclamation of Abraham Lincoln."

"I went to a private school when quite young. My father and mother died when I was nine years old. I lived then with white people, working for my board and clothes several years. While there I lacked one year of completing the high school course. I went from there to Lincoln Institute and completed the two years' Normal course. From Lincoln Institute I went to Fisk University and completed the bachelor of arts course."

"I was born on a sugar plantation; spent early life as a farmer. I had some advantages of public school instruction."

"I assisted my father on the farm and in his winter work as the town butcher during school vacations in the summer and on Saturdays. I attended the public schools of Macon, Mississippi, during their sessions of nine months. I was taught first by those whites who came from the North as teachers during the seventies; then by Fisk and Rust University graduates until I came to Fisk in 1887. I pushed my own way forward mostly, i. e. with the occasional lift my father would give when I called upon him, which I reluctantly did as he evidently had succeeded some in his teaching of self-reliance—not running up the white flag upon every occasion."

"I was born on my father's farm in the traditional log cabin. Early training was received in the country public school."

"My childhood and youth were spent in Atlanta. Most of my time I was working to help support my family. Now and then I went to night school and the summer country school. In 1876 I got desperate and broke away from my family and entered Storr's School. Finishing there in the spring of 1877, in the fall of the same year I entered Atlanta University and there I remained till I was graduated in 1884."

"I was eighteen months old, the youngest of six children, when my father died. My mother was left with a home and six children too young to work. Having nothing left me and with brothers and sisters to be supported by my mother, my early life was one of denial. I had the necessary things of life—nothing else. When I became old enough to work I secured a route on an afternoon paper and sold papers Sunday mornings. I did this all the time I was attending school in this city, making from one and a half to three and a half dollars per week. My people were free, able to read and write, and with a knowledge of refinement above the average, therefore my home surroundings were above the average. I had a good training along religious lines."

"During Vacations and holidays I worked in the shop with my father who was a wheelwright and wagon and carriage builder. I worked some with an uncle on the farm when work in the shop was slack."

"I was born in slavery and came into freedom under the terms of Lincoln's Emancipation Proclamation. While a slave I did various kinds of light work for my master's family or for other white people to whom I was often hired. From 1865 to 1867 I tried to help my mother support her large family of children. From 1867 to 1880 I was in school in Atlanta, Georgia, and Andover, Massachusetts."

"Beginning at the age of six I attended the country district school, terms averaging about two and one-half months per year. I worked on farm with my father until I was fifteen; then a few months on the railroad; but my chief work up to the age of twenty-one was in tobacco factories."

"I worked at any and all kinds of common work, such as waiting table and barber shop porter, attending the common schools and also taking advantage of such private schools as were offered."

"I was sixteen when the war closed. I learned to read and write in night school in Albany, Georgia, in 1866. I plowed all day and walked a mile and a half at night to school."

"I was born a slave on a farm in Franklin county, Virginia. When I was eight years old I walked with my parents to Kanawha county, West Virginia, a distance of two hundred and fifty miles, in the month of March. My father died when I was twelve. I never attended school until after that time."

"I was a slave until I reached the age of thirteen years. I was taken from my parents at ten years of age. I have been compelled to support myself since 1865. I had about nine months of schooling before reaching the age of twenty-one years. I have received most of my education since I became twenty-one years of age."

"I was born and reared on a farm, attended the country schools during my boyhood days. I have done all kinds of laboring work, both on the farm and on the railroad. I acted as a clerk in a supply department at a summer resort for eighteen years during summer Vacations while a student and since I have been teaching."

"I was brought up on a farm with no chance to educate myself. I had to work for what I could eat and wear, having no one to help me in life. Father was dead; mother could not help me because she was not able. I had no chance to go to school until I was nineteen years old."

"I jobbed around in summer and attended winter school, maintained by my parents; taught generally by students from Oberlin College. I was hired out as house-boy for a while; carried clothes back and forth as my mother took in washing. I was naturally studious. I studied Latin and Algebra myself. I went to Louisville, Kentucky, before the war and assisted my brother-in-law in teaching free Negro children and slaves who could get a permit. From there I went to Ohio University, Athens, Ohio, in 1849 and graduated there in 1853."

"I was educated largely by my own efforts, being left an orphan in the state of Vermont after 1865."

"My mother died when I was six months old, father when I was seven years old. Between the city and country I lived, survived and did not perish. At the age of nineteen I was janitor of graded school in Durham, North Carolina. I received ten dollars per month and my schooling. At the end of the school term I passed the fourth grade, the proudest boy in the world. I clerked in store that summer and in the fall I entered Fisk with a vim to win."

"I was born a slave. I was bound out for four years. I was taught at nights by the daughters of the man to whom I was apprenticed for four years. Lived and worked on farm most of the time till nineteen years of age."

"I was born a slave and left an orphan. I was sent adrift empty-hand without parents or guardian. I began education in night school. I entered day school under Quakers at age of seventeen. I attended two months during session for four years. Meanwhile I continued to burn the midnight oil. I became clerk, bookkeeper, deputy sheriff, policeman, public school teacher."

"I attended public schools of Augusta, Georgia, and worked between times as a newspaper carrier and later on as a printer. I was graduated from Ware High School in 1886 and then entered Atlanta University."

"I grew up on a farm with a 'scrapped up' education in fitful public and private schools and private instruction."

"My early life and training was that of the ordinary youth of our race: one of a large family of children, on a little farm, a few months' attendance every year at public schools until large enough to work. At the age of twenty I left for the North and by hard work by day and private study by night I prepared to enter Lincoln University."

"I was born a slave and was a farm boy until twenty-four years old."

"I was born in the country in Missouri. Up to nine years of age I had no schooling. I learned my A, B, C's from the Bible in my tenth year. I had two terms of school, one three months, one five months in

Missouri. My family emigrated to Nebraska when I was in my twelfth year. Farmed there and finished common and high school at Seward, Seward county, Nebraska.''

"I was a farm boy until twenty-four years of age. I was born a slave.''

"Sea life for eight or ten years. I traveled much. I attended district school in Massachusetts in winter. My academic training was received at Pierce Academy, Middleboro, Massachusetts; college work at Atlanta University.''

Women

"I attended public school in a rural district until sixteen years old. I then went to a small town and entered graded school. I made a good average with attendance daily the first term and was promoted. The next term I became tutor. My parents being dead my teachers became interested in me and made it possible for me to enter college in 1893.''

"I was reared on the farm until old enough to earn wages; then I was hired out until about twenty years old, when I entered school for the first time. Steady work and interested parties put me thru school.''

"I was reared on a farm. My parents were poor yet they kept me supplied with books and saw to it that I attended our rural school regularly. At the age of fourteen I entered Tougaloo University.''

"I was reared on a large farm owned by my father, who was one of the most extensive cotton planters in Ouachita Parish. My parents were not educated but both could read and write; and knowing the advantage of an education they spent a fortune in educating their children, giving thirteen—all who did not die in early childhood—a fair English training. When I was nine years of age they employed a tutor in the home to prepare me to be sent off to school, since educational advantages for Negroes were so poor in that part of the state. The next year I entered Straight.''

"I was born in a cabin and attended a country school.''

"The child of a college-bred mother and fairly intelligent father, my home life and early training were good; I had every opportunity and encouragement to acquire an education.''

"I had a good home and intelligent parents, who were free people before the war, hence I enjoyed some educational advantages before the Civil War. My father was a barber and a lawyer, the first colored man admitted to the bar in Tennessee. My mother was a skilled dressmaker who served for Mrs. President Polk and others high in social life.''

"I attended the public school of Oberlin, Ohio, for two years. We moved South in 1883. From then I was taught in the home until I went off to school in 1890.''

"I was a pupil in the public school of Gainesville, Florida, until about sixteen years of age. Then I entered the State Normal School at Tallahassee, Florida, from which I graduated in 1902. While a student at Tallahassee I taught each summer in rural schools. During each school year I earned my board entirely by services rendered in the president's family. After graduating I taught two consecutive terms in city schools and in 1904 spent the summer studying at the University of Chicago. In the fall of 1904 I returned South and entered Clark University."

"I was educated in Iowa. I earned my way thru the University."

"My father was a man of fair education; mother not formally educated but a great reader from her youth up. Both were actively interested in the education of their children."

Section 12. Occupations

The value of any educational scheme is seen in the life and work of the men and women who have enjoyed the opportunities afforded by the same. In estimating the value of college training for the Negroes of America it is quite natural, therefore, to ask, What are the college-bred Negro Americans doing? As a matter of fact this is the first and in some degree the crucial question asked concerning college-bred Negroes. The Conference finds that these Negro graduates are at present, with few exceptions, usefully and creditably employed and that there is an increased and pressing demand for college trained Negroes.

The statistics set forth in this section are compiled from the reports of only about one-fourth of the total number of living Negro college graduates in the United States. While not exhaustive they are of much value, since they may be regarded as typical of the whole group.

The following table compiled from the returned blanks of the Negro college graduates reporting shows the various occupations in which these graduates are engaged and the number engaged in each occupation:

OCCUPATION OF NEGRO COLLEGE GRADUATES REPORTED BY THEMSELVES

Occupation		Occupation	
Architect ..	1	Mail carriers	5
Banker	1	Matron	1
Barbers ..	3	Mechanical drawing	1
Bookkeeper	1	Merchant.	1
Bookkeeper and editor	1	Merchant and real estate dealer	1
Business	1	Miner . . .	1
Business manager of school..	1	Missionaries . .	6
Cashier in bank ..	1	Music teachers	2
Caterer	1	Newspaper correspondent	1
Census worker	1	Physicians	46
Civil engineer ..	1	Physician and druggist	2
Civil service . . .	1	Planter and real estate dealer ..	1
Clerical workers	6	Post office clerks	12
Clerk general Land Office (U. S.) . .	1	Preachers	97
Clerk Treasury Department (U. S.) . . .	1	Preacher and editor ..	2
Dean of college .	1	Preacher and farmer .	1
Dentist	2	Preacher and physician ..	1
Director of publicity and research..	1	Preacher and teacher .	47
Domestic .	1	Preceptress	2
Draftsman .	1	Preceptress and matron..	1
Draftsman (U. S.)..	1	President of bank ..	1
Dressmaker ..	1	President of college	1
Druggists	3	Railway mail service	10
Druggists and physicians ..	2	Real estate dealers	3
Editors	2	Secretaries . .	2
Editor and preacher	1	Shoe dealer . .	1
Electrical engineers .	2	Stenographers	2
Elevator operator .	1	Students	28
Farmers	6	Superintendents	4
Farmer and preacher .	1	Superintendent manual training	1
Foreman	1	Surgeon and physician . .	2
Government service ..	1	Tailor . .	2
Grocer . . .	1	Teachers	353
Housekeepers ..	6	Teacher and editor	1
Housewives ..	13	Teacher and lawyer ..	1
Insurance	2	Teacher and matron	1
Internal revenue collector ..	1	Teacher, preacher, farmer	1
Janitors ..	2	Undertaker	1
Judge ..	1	United States clerkship	2
Lawyers.	26	United States deputy marshal	1
Lawyer and teacher..	1	United States Pension Bureau	2
Librarian . . .	1	Waiters .	2
Lumber dealer	1		

It is seen from the table that the occupations which draw the largest numbers of these graduates are teaching, preaching, the practice of medicine and the practice of law. Of those reporting occupations the numbers so engaged are as follows:

OCCUPATION	Number engaged	Per cent of total reporting
Teaching	407	53.8
Preaching ..	151	20
Medicine	53	7
Law ..	29	3.8

Here indeed is shown the particular mission of the Negro college: the training of teachers and leaders and professional men and women for the black people of America. The work of the educated Negro is largely the work of leadership.

Teachers

The crying need of the four million Negroes at the close •of the Civil War showed itself in the call for teachers. In response to this call came the early Negro colleges, established primarily for the training of Negro teachers. That has been and is today their chief mission.

The above statistics show that 407 or 53.8 per cent of the total number of Negro college graduates reporting occupation are engaged in the profession of teaching. These men and women are scattered thruout the South and are engaged in teaching in all kinds of institutions—from primary to collegiate. It can be truly said that the progress of the American Negro during the forty-seven years since emancipation has been due largely to the wholesome and helpful influence of these Negro college graduates who have labored as teachers of their people.

Preachers

The Negro church and the Negro preacher have occupied a unique place in the social development of the black people of this country. Both during and since the slave regime the church has been the chief social center of the Negro people. The church and the people alike have suffered from an ignorant ministry and the end of the suffering is not yet. It is encouraging, however, to find that many educated Negroes have entered and are entering this sphere of activity. Of the number reporting occupation, 151 or 20 per cent are engaged in the ministry. This indicates to some extent the work of the Negro college in this important field and it likewise gives hope for the future.

Most of. these ministers have been trained in the Negro theological schools, chief of which are the following:

Gammon Theological Seminary, Atlanta, Georgia
Payne Theological Seminary, Wilberforce, Ohio

Virginia Union, Richmond, Virginia
Lincoln, Lincoln University, Pennsylvania
Atlanta Baptist, Atlanta, Georgia
Talladega, Talladega, Alabama
Fisk, Nashville, Tennessee

Many of these ministers have done work in theological schools of the North. Among those reporting are graduates of the following northern schools:

Yale Divinity School, New Haven, Connecticut
Andover Theological Seminary, Andover, Massachusetts
Hartford Theological Seminary, Hartford, Connecticut
Auburn Theological Seminary, Auburn, New York
Drew Theological Seminary, Madison, New Jersey
Oberlin Theological Seminary, Oberlin, Ohio
Princeton Seminary, Princeton, New Jersey
Western Theological Seminary, Allegheny, Pennsylvania
Boston University School of Theology, Boston, Massachusetts

It is encouraging to note here that most of these ministers have completed college before entering upon their theological training. The Negro ministry is rapidly changing from an uneducated to an educated factor in Negro life in America.

Physicians

The Negroes of the South are looking to the members of their own race for medical attention and so the demand for Negro physicians is great. Social conditions, too, have increased this demand. There is, therefore, an ever widening field for the Negro doctor. The above table shows that fifty-three or seven per cent of the total number reporting occupations are engaged in the practice of medicine. The influence of this profession upon the masses of Negroes cannot be overestimated. These men and women have done much to raise the physical and moral tone of the communities in which they have worked and their influence upon the cultural standards of their people has been marked. These physicians report themselves as graduates from the following medical schools:

Negro Medical Schools

Leonard Medical School, Raleigh, North Carolina
Howard Medical School, Washington, District of Columbia
Meharry Medical School, Nashville, Tennessee

Northern Medical Schools

Harvard Medical School, Boston, Massachusetts
University of Pennsylvania, Philadelphia, Pennsylvania
Albany Medical College, Albany, New York
Northwestern University Medical School, Chicago, Illinois
University of Michigan, Ann Arbor, Michigan
Chicago Medical School, Chicago, Illinois
Indiana Medical College, Indianapolis, Indiana
College of Physicians and Surgeons, Chicago, Illinois
Illinois Medical College, Chicago, Illinois
College of Physicians and Surgeons, Boston, Massachusetts
Denver Medical College, Denver, Colorado
University of Pittsburg, Pittsburg, Pennsylvania
University of Iowa, Iowa City, Iowa
Bennett Medical College, Chicago, Illinois
National Medical University, Chicago, Illinois

Lawyers

The lot of the Negro lawyer has not been on the whole a pleasant one. While the need for his services has been great he has not been given a fair chance to meet this need. Many things have militated against him. In the first place the discriminating laws of the South have so circumscribed the ordinary and customary forms of legal procedure that the Negro lawyer from the very start finds the odds against him. The very laws under which he must practice and upon which he must build his methods of procedure are in many instances aimed directly against the people from whom he must draw his clientele. In the second place the injustice which the Negro meets all too frequently in the courts of the South has made the success of the Negro lawyer all the more uncertain. With judge and jury afflicted with racial prejudice he cannot always be sure of receiving justice at their hands, even tho the evidence in the case and the accepted forms of judicial procedure seem to assure success to his efforts. Lastly, the Negro lawyer must meet the prejudice, the antipathy and the lack of confidence on the part of his own people. The latter, however, may be due largely to the conditions mentioned above. When we note the confidence placed by Negroes in their teachers, their preachers and their doctors it is only natural to presume that they would place similar confidence in the lawyers of their race did social, political and economic customs but give them an opportunity for doing so.

Nevertheless there have been many college-bred Negroes to enter the legal profession. Of the number reporting occupations, 29 or 3.8 per cent are engaged in the practice of law. The following schools of law have trained these men:

Howard University Law Department
Wilberforce University Law Department
Walden University Law Department
Allen University Law Department
Harvard University Law School
Boston University Law School
Yale University Law School
University of Minnesota Law School
Ohio State University Law School
Columbia University Law School
Kansas State University Law School
University of Michigan Law School
Chicago College of Law
Cleveland Law School
Kent Law School (Chicago)
Western Reserve University Law School
University of Iowa Law School

These lawyers are practicing in the following states:

Ohio	Massachusetts
Connecticut	Kentucky
Illinois	Tennessee
Iowa	South Carolina
Minnesota	Georgia
Kansas	Texas
Missouri	Oklahoma
Pennsylvania	District of Columbia
New York	West Virginia

The work of the Negro professional men has been and is of great importance in the educational, social and economic uplift of the Negro race in America. By precept and by example these men have taught the lessons of sacrifice and perseverance—lessons so much needed by the newly emancipated race. Likewise their example of thrift and economy cannot be overestimated; it has indeed made for progress of the Negro American.

Section 13. Ownership of Property

It is difficult to collect reliable statistics concerning the ownership of property but the results here are worth the effort. In collecting data for this study the Negro college graduates were asked the amount of land owned, the assessed value of real estate, lands and houses in their possession and the market value of total property owned.

The statistics on landownership cover the ownership of farm land and the ownership of lots and from these the following tables are compiled:

LANDOWNERS—FARM LAND

CLASS OF FARMS	*No. of owners*	*Total acreage*
Under three acres . .	45	44
Three and under 10 .	23	. 117
Ten and under 20 .	21	260
Twenty and under 50 .	36	1,179
Fifty and under 100	28	2,007
One hundred and under 175	30	3,858
One hundred and seventy-five and under 250 .	11	2,402
Two hundred and fifty and under 500 .	10	3,599
Five hundred and under 1,000 .	4	2,606
One thousand and over .	2	3,233
Total	210	19,305

LANDOWNERS—LOTS

NUMBER OF LOTS	*No. of owners*	*Total lots*
Under 5 lots . . .	150	293
Five and under 10 . .	19	113
Ten and under 15 . .	15	179
Fifteen and under 25 . .	9	157
Twenty-five and under 45 . .	2	65
Forty-five and over .	2	719
Total	197	1,526

The tables show that two hundred and ten of the graduates report the ownership of 19,305 acres of farm land, an average of ninety-two acres per graduate reporting ownership, while one hundred and ninety-seven graduates report the ownership of 1,526 lots, which is an average of eight lots per graduate reporting ownership.

The reports of assessed value of real estate, land and houses, owned by Negro college graduates reporting are com-compiled in the following table which shows total assessed value of real estate of 458 graduates reporting ownership to be $1,640,750.68 or an average of $3,582.42 per individual so reporting:

ASSESSED VALUE OF REAL ESTATE

	Number	Amount
Less than $100..	5	$ 280 00
$100–$250	11	1,770 00
$250–$500 .	25	6,757 68
$500–$1,000..	49	33,450 00
$1,000–$1,500 ..	67	73,019 00
$1,500–$2,000 ..	42	66,680 00
$2,000–$2,500 ..	46	93,970 00
$2,500–$3,000 ..	39	99,330 00
$3,000–$4,000 ..	50	157,430 00
$4,000–$5,000 ..	35	144,236 00
$5,000–$10,000	57	357,900 00
$10,000–$15,000 ..	23	252,178 00
$15,000–$20,000 .	5	80,000 00
$20,000–$30,000 ..	4	96,000 00
$30,000–$40,000 ..	5	176,850 00
Total	458	$ 1,640,750 68

Average per individual reporting $3,582.42.

The following table is compiled from the reports of total property owned by 495 graduates reporting and shows a total of $2,794,537 or an average of $5,645.53 per individual:

TOTAL PROPERTY

	Number	Amount
Less than $500	26	$ 7,180
$500–$1,000.	40	27,035
$1,000–$1,500 ..	43	46,782
$1,500–$2,000 ..	43	68,250
$2,000–$3,000 ..	78	177,850
$3,000–$4,000 ..	60	190,900
$4,000–$5,000 ..	40	165,500
$5,000–$7,500 ..	64	370,000
$7,500–$10,000	25	203,450
$10,000–$15,000 ..	30	322,890
$15,000–$20,000 ..	18	288,800
$20,000–$25,000 ..	9	188,900
$25,000–$30,000 ..	6	153,000
$30,000–$40,000 ..	7	228,000
$40,000–$50,000 ..	3	126,000
$50,000–$100,000 . .	2	110,000
More than $100,000..	1	120,000
Total	495	$ 2,794,537

Average per individual reporting $5,645.53.

It is difficult to estimate from these meagre statistics the amount of property in the possession of the Negro college graduates. In the first place many who are known to be in possession of property did not make answer to these questions and so are not included in the above tables. Then, too, the usual ratio between assessed value and real value taken into consideration here alters the figures to the advantage of the whole group. Lastly, it must be remembered that the total replies to the conference questionnaire cover only about one-fourth of the total number of living Negro college graduates. All things taken into consideration it is probably safe to say that the college-bred Negro Americans are in possession of $15,000,000 worth of property.

Some conclusions may be drawn from this phase of the study:

1. The Negro college graduates have made and are making a good showing in the accumulation of property, both personal and real estate.

2. By precept and by example these men and women are teaching their people the virtues of thrift, economy and saving.

3. No small measure of the value of these men and women may be seen in the impetus they have given to their people in the building of homes and the accumulation of property.

Section 14. Avocations

The work of the educated Negro is largely the work of leadership. The college-bred Negro, therefore, finds great opportunity for telling activity among his people and that in addition to his regular vocation. A study of the avocations of these educated men and women reveals much of interest and shows in a striking way the place of the college-bred in the Negro race. In like manner it gives some idea of the social value of the college-bred Negro to America.

Learned Societies

The Negro college graduates have reported themselves as members of the following learned societies:

Academy of Science, St. Louis
African Society (London)

Alpha Kappa Literary
Alpha Phi Alpha   .
American Academy for Advancement of Science
American Academy of Political and Social Science
American Archæological Association
American Association of Electrical Engineers
American Breeders' Association
American Civic Alliance
American Economic Association
American Geographic Society
American Historical Association
American Institute for Psychic Research
American Library Association
American Medical Association
American Nature Study Society
American Negro Academy
American Ornithologists' Union
American Philological Association
American Statistical Association
Arkansas Medical, Dental and Pharmaceutical Surgical Association
Association of Collegiate Alumnæ
Chicago Medical Society
Classical Association of the South and Middle West
Constitution League
Eastern Manual Training Association
Entomological Society of America
Illinois Academy of Science
Illinois State Medical Society
Inter-State Literary Society of Kansas and the West
Massachusetts Medical Society
Medical Society, Essex County, New Jersey
National Bar Association
National Educational Association
National Medical Association
National Sociological Society
Niagara Movement
Phi Beta Kappa
Physics Club of Indiana University
Rock City Academy of Medicine and Surgery
Sigma Chi Fraternity (Chicago Chapter)
Society of Arts (England)   .
Standard Literary Society, Chicago
State Medical Association (Tennessee), Colored

Publications

The college-bred Negro has contributed in a small way to the literature of America. In this contribution we find some works of considerable importance whether viewed from the standpoint of literature, or history, or science, or sociology. We find also, in addition to the larger publications, numerous pamphlets, essays and smaller works of importance such as those issued by the American Negro Academy, the Committee of Twelve for the Advancement of the Negro Race, the different religious organizations and numerous individuals.

The official organ of each of the leading Negro religious bodies is directed in large part by college-bred men.

Almost all of the leading magazines have published articles written by Negro college graduates—the *Atlantic*, the *Forum*, the *North American Review*, the *World's Work*, the *Century*, the *Independent*, the *Outlook*. Something has been done in the field of poetry as is evidenced by James W. Johnson's "O Black and Unknown Bards" and "Mother Night"; by Kelly Miller's "Mors Vincta" and "A Moral Axiom"; and by Silas Xavier Floyd's "Floyd's Flowers" and "Not by Bread Alone."

Atlanta University Publication, Number 14, Efforts for Social Betterment among Negro Americans, gives a list of newspapers and magazines which have been published by Negroes. Many of these have been controlled wholly or in part by college-bred men.

The following bibliography, by no means exhaustive, is some indication of the literary activity of the college-bred Negro American:

Anderson, Matthew. Presbyterianism and its Relation to the Negro. Philadelphia, 1897. 12mo., 263 pp.

Barber, J..M. One Hundred One Eminent Negroes.

Bowen, J. W. E. Sermons. Philadelphia. 88 pp.
Africa and the American Negro. Atlanta. 250 pp.
Addresses. Atlanta. 300 pp.

Brawley, B. G. The Negro in Literature and Art. 1910.

Broughton, Mrs. J. A. O. Women's Work. 52 pp.
Twenty Years' Experience of a Missionary. 140 pp.
Christian Homes the Hope of the Race.

Byrd, W. A. Reply to German Criticism on Bible. 30 pp.
Exposition of Kinosis. 50 pp.
Commentary on Joel. 30 pp.
Camphor, Rev. A. P. Missionary Story Sketches and Folk Lore from Africa. 346 pp. Cincinnati and New York.
Camphor, Rev. R. A. Papers and Addresses. 50 pp. Atlanta.
Coffin, A. O. A Land without Chimneys. Cincinnati. 352 pp.
Cooper, A. J. A Voice from the South. Xenia, O., 1892. 30 pp.
Crogman, W. H. Talks for the Times. Atlanta. 330 pp.
Crummell, Alexander. Africa and America. Springfield, Mass., 1891. 466 pp.
Du Bois, W. E. B. Suppression of the Slave Trade. New York, 1896. 335 pp. (Harvard Historical Series, No. 1.)
The Philadelphia Negro. Philadelphia, 1899. 520 pp.
The Souls of Black Folk. Chicago, 1903. 264 pp.
John Brown. Philadelphia, 1909. 406 pp.
Editor Atlanta University Studies of the Negro Problem.
Dyson, Walter H. Syllabus on U. S. History and Civics. Washington, 1910.
Floyd, S. X. Life of C. T. Walker.
Gospel of Service and other Sermons.
Floyd's Flowers.
National Perils.
Gilmer, John C. History of Alabama.
A Guide to English Oration.
Gregory, J. M. Frederick Douglass. Springfield, Mass., 1890. 300 pp.
Grimke, A. H. William Lloyd Garrison. (American Reformers Series.) New York, 1891. 405 pp.
Charles Sumner. (American Reformers Series.) New York, 1892. 515 pp.
Grimke, F. J. The Negro, his Rights and Wrongs. Washington, D. C., 1899. 100 pp.
Henderson, G. W. Essays on Negro Citizenship.
Plantation Life in Louisiana.
Hubert, J. W. *Syllabi:*
(1) Seven Studies in Physiography.
(2) Seven Studies in Right Living.
(3) Seven Studies in Geology.
(4) Life's Ten Richest Blessings.
Johnson, C. J. Pilgrimage of a Race. 1910.
Kealing, H. T. History of African Methodism in Texas.
Fortune Telling in History.
The Minor Prophets.
How to Live Longer.
Langston, J. M. From the Virginia Plantations. Hartford, 1894. 544 pp.

Lawson, Jesse. How Solve the Race Problem. Washington, D. C. 297 pp.

Ethics of the Labor Problem. Washington, D. C. 14 pp.

Lewis, W. H. A Primer of College Foot-ball. New York. 205 pp.

Long, F. A. Across the Continent. Danville, Va. 60 pp.

Lovinggood, R. S. Why *hic, haec, hoc* for the Negro? Marshall, Tex., 1900. 56 pp.

The Negro Seer, his Mission and Preparation.

McWilliams, B. F. The Needs of the Negro. Univ. Press, Richmond. 1903. 16mo.

The Negro Church of Virginia, its Condition and Needs. 1905.

Miller, Albert P. The Black Man's Burden or the Two Sides of the Negro Problem.

Miller, Kelly. The Education of the Negro. Washington, 1902.

Race Adjustment. New York and Washington, 1908. 306 pp.

Mossell, C. W. Toussant L'Ouverture.

Ousley, B. F. Gospels and Acts translated into African Tongue. New York. 371 pp.

Paisley, J. W. The Voice of Mezraim. New York. 122 pp.

Payne, D. A. History of the A. M. E. Church. Nashville, 1891. 498 pp.

Paynter, J. H. Joining the Navy. Hartford. 330 pp.

Pegues, A. W. Our Baptist Ministers and Schools. Springfield, Ohio. 680 pp.

Pettus, J. W. Home Again. Fort Smith, Ark. 34 pp.

Vagaries of Substitute. Indianapolis. 127 pp.

Phillips, C. H. History of the Colored Methodist Episcopal Church.

Scarborough, W. S. First Greek Lessons. New York. 150 pp.

Birds of Aristophanes. Boston.

Scruggs, L. A. Afro-American Women of Distinction. Raleigh, N. C.

Sinclair, William A. The Aftermath of Slavery. Boston, 1905. 358 pp.

Talbert, H. The Sons of Allen. 286 pp.

Turner, C. H. Numerous biological publications, the result of scientific research.

Work, F. J. New Jubilee Songs. Nashville, 1902. 50 pp.

Folk Songs of American Negro. Nashville. 64 pp.

Some American Negro Folk Songs. Boston, 120 pp.

Among the interesting pamphlets published by Negro college graduates are the following:

Bruce, Roscoe Conkling. Service by the Educated Negro.

Carver, G. W. Bulletin of Tuskegee Experiment Station.

Cook, C. C. Study of the Negro Problem.

Crummell, Alexander. Sermons and Addresses.

Dammond, W. H. Factoring.

Davis, M. T. The South the Negro's Door of Hope (An Essay).

The Education of Negro Youth of Texas.

Grimke, A. H.   Why Disfranchisement is Bad.

Harris, Eugene.   Social Purity.

McClellan, G. W.   Poems.   Nashville.

Miller, Kelly.   A Review of Hoffman's "Race Traits and Tendencies,"
    etc.   Washington, 1897.   36 pp.

    As to the Leopard's Spots, etc.   Washington, 1905.

    The Primary Need of the Negro Race.   Washington, 1899.   18 pp.

    The Political Capacity of the Negro.

Steward, T. G.   Black St. Domingo Legion.

Talley, T. W.   A Natural Trinity.

Wesley, A. A.   The Spanish-American War.

Williams, D. H.   Reports of Surgical Cases.

Wright, R. R.   Historical Sketch of Negro Education in Georgia.   Sa-
    vannah.   58 pp.

Public Office

The following is a partial list of public offices which have been held by Negro college graduates:

Seven Alderman (N. C., Pa., Mass., Ky., S. C.)

Nine Members Board of Education (N. C., S. C., Ohio, Tenn., D. C., Ga., Kan.)

Two Assistant Attorney Generals (N. Y.)

Members of State Legislatures (N. C., Miss., Ill., Ga., Tenn., Minn.)

Four Clerks in District Courts (Kan., Okla., D. C.)

One Member of Congress

Three served in Spanish-American War (Major and Paymaster, Chaplain, and Captain)

Two Judges of Civil Courts

Two United States Deputies

Four Tax Assessors (Ill., Ark., Miss., N. C.)

Five Officials in Custom Houses (La., Tenn., Va., Ga.)

Two State Superintendents of Public Instruction (La., Ala.)

Two Medical Inspectors (Pa., Col.)

One Special Land Agent

One City and State Health Officer (Col.)

Assistant Corporation Counsel (New York City)

Inspector of Customs

Member of Grand Jury (Ark.)

United States Jail Physician

Justice of Peace

Deputy Auditor

Engrossing Clerk, General Assembly

Deputy Collector of Customs (La.)

Prosecuting Attorney (Ill.)

Secretary of Haytian Legation
Tax Collector (Pa.)
Chaplain House of Representatives (S. C.)
Registrar of Births and Deaths (West Indies)
Registrar of Deposits, U. S. Mint (La.)
United States Minister to Hayti
United States Minister to Liberia
Assistant United States District Attorney (Mass.)

Charitable Work

The Atlanta University Publication, Number 14, Efforts for Social Betterment among Negro Americans, gives an elaborate account of the charitable work being done by the Negroes of this country. The field is broad and the phases of this activity are many: church, school, general charity, women's clubs, old folk's homes, orphanages, hospitals, young men's Christian associations, young women's Christian associations, refuges and homes for women and children, libraries, day nurseries, social settlements, kindergartens, civic reform.

The college bred Negroes have done and are doing a large share of the work along these charitable lines. The following list shows in a general way the charitable activity of these men and women:

Church work	Old folks' homes
Y. M. C. A. and Y. W. C. A.	Hospitals
Trustees of institutions	Labor organizations
Anti-tuberculosis leagues	Boys' reform societies
Charitable societies	Jail and slum work
Day nurseries	Temperance and prohibition move-
Social settlements	ment
Secret societies	White Cross society
Prison reform	American Health League
Mission work	Jeanes Fund
Play grounds	Associated charities
Civic leagues	Libraries
Mothers' clubs	Social reform

The following extracts from reports received will show something of the charitable work of individual graduates:

Originator of movement to investigate sanitary conditions of our people in New Orleans.

Home for friendless girls, Washington, D. C.

Associated Charities, Washington, D. C.

Work in slums of Providence, R. I.

Member of Oberlin Improvement Society.

Entire time in connection with —— College devoted to relieving needy students and promoting the welfare of the institution. Actual money given $3,967.90.

United Charities for Colored People, Nashville, Tenn.

Vice-president North Carolina Reform School Association.

Chairman of Negro branch of Associated Charities, Gallipolis, Ohio.

Member of board of directors National Home-finding Society and of Library and Improvement Association; member of Anti-tuberculosis Committee, of Play Ground Association, of Colored Orphan Society, Louisville, Ky.

Working girls' home, Columbia, S. C.

United Charities, Rochester, N. Y.

Member of board of directors of State Orphan Society, Oxford, N. C.

Member Associated Charities, Raleigh, N. C.

Association for Protection of Colored Women; Old Ladies' and Orphans' Home, Memphis, Tenn.

Home for Aged Men; Association for Prevention of Tuberculosis; Trustee of Mutual Housing Company, the object of which is the improvement of housing conditions in Springfield, Mass., and vicinity.

Volunteer work in connection with probation officer of the juvenile court of St. Louis, Mo.

Member of Consolidated Charities of New Albany, La.

Secretary of Galveston Relief Association.

Trustee of Orphan and Old Ladies' Home; chairman Domestic Science Board; Association for Relief of Colored Women; organizer social settlement work, Memphis, Tenn.

Negro school improvement league; Teachers' and Citizens' Co-operative Association; social settlement, Petersburg, Va.

Superintendent of Mercy Hospital, Nashville, Tenn.

Member of Committee for Improving Industrial Conditions among Negroes in New York City; member of N. A. A. C. P.

Colored Orphan Home, Huntsville, Ala.

Chairman board of directors of Provident Hospital and Training School for Negroes, Arkansas.

President of Galveston Relief Association.

United Charities, Nashville, Tenn.

Civic Improvement Club; Farmers' Union and Protective League, Okmulgee, Okla.

Associated Charities; Director of Slater Hospital, Winston, N. C.

Secretary Civic League; Board of Directors of Anti-tuberculosis League, Portsmouth, Va.

Secretary Social Uplift Society for Colored People, Jersey City, N. J.

Built the Pickford Sanitorium for Tuberculous Negroes, Southern Pines, N. C.

Editor and Investigator Atlanta University Publications; member of Committee of Forty, N. A. A. C. P.; American Secretary Universal Races Congress.

Director of Public Play Grounds for Colored Youths; Volunteer Probation Officer of Juvenile Court; Association for Prevention of Tuberculosis, St. Louis, Mo.

Trustee of Amanda Smith Industrial Home; Probation Officer, Cook county, Ill.

President Board of Managers for Reform School for Girls, Kansas.

Legal and general adviser of the Cleveland Home for Aged Colored People; Probation Officer of Juvenile Court of Cuyahoga county, Ohio. (No compensation.)

Director of the Sarah Ann White Home for Aged and Infirm Colored People, Washington, D. C.

Organizer of state teachers' association; organizer fair association; organizer colored anti-tuberculosis league, Georgia.

State Superintendent of Department of Anti-narcotics, W. C. T. U., North Carolina.

Trustee of Provident Hospital and Training School for Negroes, Chicago; director of Douglass Center, Chicago; director of Juvenile Court League, No. 4, Chicago; trustee Peace Haven Institute, Blackville, S. C. Personal work. For the past eight years I have been assisting Negro physicians in the establishment of infirmaries of their own thruout the South and instructing them along surgical lines.

Old Folks' Home, Selma, Ala.

Associated Charities, Augusta, Ga.

Colored Orphan Home, Columbus, Ohio.

Business

The Negro college graduates report themselves as engaged in the following business enterprises, in almost every case in addition to the regular vocation:

Real estate .	. 38	Merchandise . .	4
Banking . .	19	Home association .	1
Drug business .	5	Plumbing	1
Shoe business . .	3	Newspaper business	5
Gardener . '	1	Trust company .	3
Farming	8	Mining company	6
Building and loan association	. 11	Contractor	1
Editors . . .	5	Insurance .	4
Construction	2	Coal business .	1
Co-operative business league	1	Fair association	1
Land improvement .	4	Publishing	3
Investment .	4	Grocers	2
Fruit farming .	2	Millinery . .	1
Warehouse . .	1	Steam laundering . .	1
Manufacturing	4	Mercantile company	1
Cotton ginning	2	Realty company . .	3
Lumber business .	1	General store business	1
Book store	1	Printing . . .	2
Mail order . .	1	Poultry raising .	2
Music publisher .	2		

Section 15.   Education of Children

How shall you educate your children? The answers received in reply to this question are interesting. By far the greater number of those making reply are planning to give their children the advantages of a college education, hoping thereby to properly equip them for life's work, whether in the trades or in the professions. Many of these answers are grouped as follows:

College	. 101
College and professional . .	. 101
Trade, college and professional .	48
College training and trade	45
According to their ability . .	44
According to their inclination .	41
Professional	24
College, trade or professional .	20
Industrial and professional	9
Trade	7
College or professional	3
Some industrial and some college	2
Academic and trade	2
Technical	1
Head, hand and heart .	1
Liberal education	1
College and professional or business .	1
Professional or trade	1
College and business	1
Literary education and domestic work	1
Academic . .	1

The following quotations, none of which is included in the above grouping, are taken from the replies to this question concerning the education of children:

"It is my present intention to give my boys a full university training in order that they may be equipped to take high rank in whatever calling or profession they may choose."

"I believe in educating the child to make the best citizen; a college education to those who will take it."

"In obedience to their inclinations and gifts and without prejudice for or against any particular training. Technical, agricultural, mercantile, professional training are of equal importance if preparation and research are sufficient, there being urgent need for real high grade leadership in every avenue for the Negro. If then any offspring from my household manifest special taste for and high merit in any worthy line, I shall only ask God to enable me to assist them to the highest in that line."

"First public school, secondly college, third university, then if possible provide for her to study abroad. I shall teach the importance of attainment of the highest possible type of culture and refinement and the importance of possessing something that people who have money want."

"I have but one daughter. I plan to give her a college education in southern, eastern and European institutions."

"I am striving to be in shape to give my children a thoro, practical education which will best fit them for the daily pursuits of life."

"I shall endeavor to give that training which in my judgment will be of the highest good to him."

"I want my daughter to make music her specialty but will allow her to choose her literary course."

"Each is to receive at least a normal and academic education. Two or three may take the university course, one in music, one in theology."

"It is my intention to give them the very best education that they can assimilate."

"I desire to have them brought up at a school such as Fisk after they have reached puberty and later at a northern university. But first of all I shall teach them the fundamentals of politeness, hygiene, and the art of doing work assigned them smoothly and with polish."

"The education of my children will probably depend largely upon their own wishes but I should like them to receive training equivalent to the four years' college course at Atlanta University and professional or special training for some particular line of work."

"If I should be so fortunate as to have any children I would send them to Phillips Exeter, Harvard and Lawrence Scientific School."

"Some in trade, some in college and some in a profession. One is already a dressmaker, another is a trained nurse and still another has finished in theology and is doing good pastoral work at Albany, Georgia."

"I expect to send my boys thru college and my daughter thru a normal training school."

"I propose to give them as complete an education as they can receive."

"As their talent seems to indicate. The best is none too good. Broadly as men and as American citizens and not narrowly as Negroes."

"I dont know as to a trade or a profession but most certainly I shall give my boy a college education and my daughter a good normal training."

"College and technical as far as my influence can bring this about; ultimately, of course, the child must decide."

"This would depend largely upon the natural tendency of the children but my desire would be for them to have a college education and, if possible, for the boys to take a profession afterwards. Both boys and girls should work at some trade during vacation seasons while in public school as I believe no boy or girl should be permitted to grow up without learning how to do some kind of work proficiently with the hands."

"I favor college education because then they are better prepared to succeed; then to his trade or profession well equipped."

"I shall give them a higher Christian literary education as a foundation and allow them afterwards to study any trade or profession they may wish."

"I shall educate my girls to be school teachers."

"I am giving my son academic and professional and my daughter academic and trade."

"In the way that shall best fit them as individuals to be of greatest service to themselves and to others. I desire them to have a three-fold education."

"Train their early years in some form of handicraft or trade; give them a college course in an institution for Negroes; and the boys a professional course in one of the best schools without regard to color."

"I will try to educate my children according to their inclinations. I am not partial; to any kind of education which fits men and women for true service."

"For profession if they show inclination and ability sufficient to indicate that they will be successful in such work. For trades or business if they show special adaptability for that class of work."

"I would give him a broad and comprehensive college training and leave it to his own inclination as to trade or profession."

"I shall endeavor to study the aptitude of the child. If he or she is best fitted for an industrial life or a profession I desire to root that industry or profession into a fertile, college-trained brain."

"Boys to a trade or a profession, according to their respective inclinations and apparent adaptability. Girls in college and domestic science."

"Some trade along with their preparatory training. College course, a part of which shall be in some Christian institution. Their professional training shall be the outgrowth of their natural adaptation together with the aid and direction of parents."

"Intend to make teachers of some of them. The boys wish to be scientific farmers."

"In college and in the ministry with some industrial training, with the hope that he may become a missionary to Africa."

"Intend to make a dentist of my boy and a musician of my girl."

"Hope to have them learn trade, go thru one of the northern colleges and learn some profession."

"Boy, to trade or medicine; girl, to domestic science and music."

"I am striving to give my children a thoro practical education which will best fit them for the daily pursuits of life."

Section 16. Hindrances

What have been your chief hindrances? Most of the hindrances which were reported in the replies to this question find a place in the following grouping:

1. Lack of money.
2. Race prejudice against the Negro.
3. Prejudice of Negroes themselves.

The following quotations are taken from the replies:

"Prejudice has all along hindered me in getting what I have merited. On the other hand, it has been a negative good, doing for me in some measure what a rough sea does for a mariner: bringing out whatever of good stuff there is in me."

"My chief hindrance has been a lack of funds. I have always had to hustle for what I have attained and having become accustomed to it I hardly consider that a hindrance now. I have found a certain amount of prejudice everywhere I have been but I have also found that ambition and energy with integrity can override prejudice."

"I have no reason to complain. While opportunities for the young Negro are fewer than for the young white man in this country, the young men of our race are neglecting opportunities which would seem golden to the young men of other lands."

"I find that a desire to work, when based on a good foundation, educational and moral, is appreciated and encouraged by all classes of people."

"My chief hindrance has been a lack of capital with which to carry out my plans. Prejudice cuts very little figure in the business world if you have what the white man wants or if he can use you in any way. He will look you up."

"I think sometimes people of our own race who are in position to do so throw obstacles in your way of progress. I think to a certain extent I have been such a victim."

"In getting into close, vital relation with my people in order to be of real service."

"I could say poverty; but it has been the spur that made me move when I would have fallen by the wayside. Prejudice and lack of opportunity: I cannot be harsh on either. Where prejudice existed I strove to soften by acquaintance and have never failed. Opportunity: so far I have always been able to be ready when it made its appearance to step in and get my share."

"Poor salary. Prejudice on account of progress and satisfactory conditions of my surroundings."

"Prejudice has militated against increase of salary in service of city."

"Prejudice has been a great hindrance but not any more so than is usual with colored people. My greatest hindrance has been lack of opportunity as I have had to meet heavy obligations since leaving school."

"Lack of opportunity thru prejudice both among the more ignorant of my race as well as among the white people has been a great hindrance to my advancement. I have never been able to receive pay adequate to my qualifications."

"Southern prejudice has helped rather than hindered me."

"Prejudice has been a great hindrance. The things which would tend to advancement for white men have been overlooked in my case on account of color."

"The same every colored man meets. Menial positions; poor pay as a teacher; fidelity to my race, which led me to decline a high position on a railroad in Georgia which I could have had by passing for white. I could get only about two-thirds the salary paid to a white teacher of the same grade."

"While I have no great complaint to make, I think perhaps my life would have been larger and far different but for my color, tho the fact that I was elected to public office in a white community shows that I have escaped much of the race prejudice with which the race has to contend.''

"The lack of money has been one of the drawbacks in my case. I never allowed prejudice to worry me. I always attended to my own business and let other people do the same."

"My opportunities have been very good. I have often been able to cross the bounds set by prejudice."

"I have not had access to hospital and clinical facilities to keep up and perfect myself in my professional work."

"Prejudice has hindered me from becoming head physician here. I am oldest in point of location here."

"I have never allowed prejudice to crush me. With me it has been more of a stimulus. It is an awful fact and works with a maliciousness that is wilful and premeditated but it is wanting in substance; it is not founded on the rock of reason and truth. It is unthinking and blind and will, therefore, ultimately work its own destruction."

"Chief hindrance perhaps is my desire to always draw salary rather than take chance in business. Prejudice has made me less prominent as an engineer, kept me from good paying positions and forced me to accept less pay for the same work. All of my classmates who are white are drawing larger salaries than I."

"Doing same or more work for less money than my white comrades. No incentive to be anything better than what I am. Difficulty in obtaining promotion over white competitors or even along with them."

"Prejudice among colored people against their own college men is a hindrance."

"I have gone steadily on and have done whatever has been my duty so far as I have been able to see my duty. I have not been directly hindered in my work, hence prejudice has hindered me in a general way in proportion as it has impeded my race."

"I have succeeded fairly well in my profession but have been prevented from reaching that prominence in it which I might have otherwise reached by the awful race prejudice that exists here as elsewhere. Then the colored lawyer does not have the stimulus to exertion the white lawyer has because he knows the honors and emoluments of the profession are denied him because of his race. No matter what his excellence or fitness he can never reach the bench or have retainers from large corporations. The truth is that the colored lawyer to succeed at all must be far beyond the average white lawyer."

"Prejudice circumscribed the sphere of activities for broader culture and for increased efficiency."

"Race prejudice has undoubtedly lessened my opportunities but on the other hand has served indirectly to make me use such opportunities as I have had to a better advantage than I would otherwise have done possibly."

"Lack of means to procure needed facilities to carry out and plan my line of work for myself and for my pupils. A desire on the part of school boards to restrict us in our efforts to secure a sufficient number of, and capable, efficient teachers, well equipped laboratories and libraries. I taught physics and chemistry in a laboratory in ———— furnished by ourselves."

"In some places silent opposition to Negro college graduates on the part of white and colored."

"Prejudice is always present but I have found far more opportunity than prejudice, i. e. prejudice that hindered in any vital sense. The greatest hindrance is the indifference of my own people to the necessity for unity and increased, well-directed activity. Prejudice has made me work harder and so has proved many times a blessing in disguise."

"It is my belief that prejudice is a spur to serious endeavor on the part of intelligent colored men."

"Prejudice and proscription have operated to my disadvantage to the extent of cooling ardor and chilling aspiration."

"Prejudice and lack of opportunity have retarded my progress but by industry, economy, conservatism and perseverance I have in a measure overcome them."

"Prejudice against the higher education of Negroes."

"Prejudice denies us the privilege of enjoying the confidence and association of many superior minds. It has denied me the opportunity to enjoy or be benefited by the large number of programs and meetings of a public or semi-public nature where a great deal of information and inspiration may be obtained."

"My chief hindrance has been lack of opportunity. There is not enough business among colored people to employ their young men and women when they finish school."

"It is hard to specify the ways in which prejudice has worked against one. No man who has been hampered by or has been compelled to contend against prejudice has been able to reach his best and biggest self."

"Prejudice has been from the very beginning the chief hindrance in my life. I have been turned from printing establishments because of objection to my color. I have been engaged for clerical work and then discharged when my color became known. It has operated against me in oratorical contests at college."

"I cannot complain of lack of opportunity. I find the old adage holds true: Where there is a will there is a way."

"Prejudice has been no barrier when it came to acquiring property, but it often crushes my spirit."

"In my estimation my chief hindrance has been that I have never had all the equipment which I felt should be mine to make the greatest possible success in the tasks which have been mine. Tho measurably successful in all my career I have so often felt the need of more mastery over the immediate problem or business. Prejudice has had to do with my life and experience as with others. Promotions which would have been given freely and early to a man of another racial identity, I have had to labor long for. Yet in all fairness I must say that whereas prejudice, damnable and low, is continually operating against me, yet I have won so far. I have got what I went after, after a fight nevertheless, yet I got it."

"I cannot buy or rent respectable property without the greatest embarrassment and sometimes not even then. This gives a set-back to my dignity and influence."

"Prejudice has closed several doors of opportunity along the line of educational advantages; was responsible for a low wage for some years; and caused much embarrassment in ways whose name is legion."

"My chief hindrance has been the treachery and vanity of the namby-pamby Negro. To put it another way my chief hindrance has been my inability to play the hypocrite."

"Prejudice is the chief hindrance in the way of all college-bred Negro men who want to make the most of life. Prejudice, I think, has made me suspicious of all white people, sometimes with injustice to them, I fear, and with injury to myself."

"My chief hindrance is that I am deprived of the enjoyment of my rights as a free citizen."

"I feel that only half the measure of the possibilities of my career has been filled because prejudice has been a handicap to the full and free prosecution of my professional labors. Most of the Negroes believe that to succeed in our courts they must have a white advocate."

"There is in this community a kindly growing sentiment on the part of the whites toward the colored people and so prejudice does not interrupt much. My chief hindrance is due to the fact that it is difficult to get my own people to appreciate in a large way our opportunities for growth and power."

"Lack of confidence among our people to intrust their business with one another and to do business with each other generally. I might term it 'race pride.' I think it is due more to absolute ignorance. However, we are coming to a better understanding of each other and business confidence in each other is being developed both on account of oppression and prejudice and the preaching of self-help among ourselves."

"Prejudice and lack of opportunity have been at once my handicap and my constant stimulant. Daily experience with them has kept me keyed up to constant exertion and the doing of my best. Expecting no quarter it has been with me a fight to the finish and a point of manhood and honor to succeed."

"Lack of proper aspiration among the masses. Failure of the people to appreciate real ability. Jealousy and prejudice among certain leaders."

"My greatest hindrance was lack of public school opportunity early in life. A lot of good time was lost in those days."

"Prejudice hinders a man all the time and everywhere in doing a man's work. No man can do his best while hampered by senseless prejudice."

"Prejudice of ignorant blacks as well as whites does a great deal to hinder. The uneducated black is very jealous of his educated brother and will do lots to hinder his progress."

"In my work I have felt perhaps more than anything else the prohibition from public library facilities in such a city as Atlanta."

"Prejudice has played so small a part that it can be considered a negligible quantity. Perhaps I have not followed the paths in which one would meet it so keenly. My chief hindrance has possibly come from within: the ignorance of the big opportunities that await the average young Negro man of education and energy in the business world provided he works eternally."

"A very limited field to choose positions from, as compared to many of my white fellow students whose academic standing was below mine. Social conditions in my home state shut me out of the career I would have naturally sought there."

"Prejudice has made me fight the harder to overcome the disabilities of caste. It has kept me alive and made me yearn to accomplish something, nerved me to live and endure suffering and sorrow of any kind in order to see the ultimate triumph of righteous civic ideals."

"Rather difficult to answer as I have worked all the while under conditions that I saw little hope of changing hence gave little thot to what I might have done under different conditions. I feel sure the lack of opportunity for full exercise of ability in certain lines has, perhaps in some cases unconsciously, served to stifle ambition and prevent activity that might have been useful to communities in which I have lived. In some instances I think prejudice has nerved me to more persistent effort."

"The color line has prevented a chance for scientific and literary work."

"Race prejudice prevents me being retained as counsel where otherwise I would be employed. It keeps away the most remunerative class of business. It compels me to accept a smaller fee for work done and services rendered than would otherwise be the case. It often causes me to contest in court for fees after they have been earned, when but for the 'previous condition of servitude' of my ancestors said fees would be cheerfully paid. No one is able to estimate the damage inflicted upon him by the forces which make for ostracism and which impose a perennial and continued boycott because of race."

"1. Prejudice which debars me from work in institutions for which my training fits me.

"2. Superficially trained Negroes who, like the dog in the manger, have ever tried to hinder my progress.

"3. The false notion that the Negro scholar does not deserve as much pay for intellectual work as a white man does for the same work.

"4. Poor salary which has made it necessary for me to abandon many of my researches at an early stage. Indeed what little I have accomplished has been at the expense of the comforts and often of the necessities of life."

Section 17. Philosophy of Life

What is your present practical philosophy in regard to the Negro race in America? This question was asked the Negro college graduates and to it varying answers were received. The following quotations are taken from the replies and are indicative of the attitude of the Negro American of college training:

"The hope of the Negro is a Christian education of heart, head and hand."

"In my opinion the Negro needs nothing so much as to be let alone. He wants not special attention either in the legislative hall or out. He wants to be treated and regarded as an American citizen in fact. He asks for no more than he merits but he wants all he does merit. To reach this point he must contend for all the term implies. Life is a battle and every man must be a fighter. Playing the baby-act will not accomplish anything. Brave men will not only suffer hardships in maintaining their rights but will face dangers. Long since I came to the conclusion that right living on our part would not alone solve the problem. It is not the worthless, ignorant spendthrift among us that arouses the white man's opposition, repression, oppression and prejudice. That class knows 'his place.'"

"I have an abiding hope for the future of the race. But great suffering and loss are in store for the race thru error. There is an attempt in a large part of the country to establish a caste system of education for the Negro.   In the state institutions they are taking out the higher studies and promoting mediocre men and women, paying them in proportion much larger salaries than they are paying college-bred Negro teachers."

"I firmly believe that the destiny of the American Negro lies largely in his own hands. I have never yet seen a self-respecting, honest and industrious Negro, educated or uneducated, who did not have the respect and good-will of the better class of whites with whom he comes in contact.   I believe that we as individuals must take as our weapons honesty, industry and economy and wage a war against prejudice."

"The Negro race in America is fortunate. The country is still far from being developed or crowded. Tho race prejudice is rampant it is still too weak to suppress any class which has the determination to rise. There is still plenty of room. Less complaint and more effort will pull us up with the dominant class. We should seek and develop all the thinly settled parts of this country."

"The Negro must continue to contend for all the rights, privileges and opportunities accorded other American citizens. He must be unyielding in this respect. He ought to ally himself with any political party that will further these ends."

"I feel that the Negro has many reasons to be hopeful. Of course there are many things that are deplorable; but on the other hand there are so many opportunities already open to us that we do not take advantage of that we would do well to spend less time in finding fault and complaining and use that time preparing ourselves for larger activities and more usefulness."

"My own confident hope is that there will be ultimately a satisfactory issue to all present race difficulties."

"I regard it as essential that political privileges be granted to men regardless of color, the same qualifications demanded of all in an absolutely impartial manner. I regard education as indispensable and believe in absolutely equal facilities for it.   .   .   The problem of the American Negro is difficult to solve upon a basis of perpetual segregation. It is particularly desirable that there shall be no segregation in the higher institutions of learning. Industrial and manual activities should be elements in the course of study for colored people as for all people but not the only elements nor even the principal ones. I think that the colored people should be stimulated to acquire property and to become fixed in their communities. In order that this may happen it is necessary to secure for the Negro greater protection of life and property."

"With education and the right to vote—for both of which the Negro must work and fight daily—he will win the place which is his here in America."

"Persistent, definite and determined effort along all legitimate lines of education, coupled with an all-controlling desire to stick to the right, will not only win for the Negro the respect of America but will give him a place immortal in the history of the world."

"Educate him in the highest and best way possible so as to enable him to successfully compete with every other element of Americanism in every walk of life."

"The accumulation of property will do more to relieve the American Negro of many hardships and disadvantages than any other agency. This should not be the case but it is. The ability to think well (generally the result of thoro training) should outrank the ability to live well (the result of accumulated wealth). First train the mind; then in order to be highly regarded by Americans own some of the world's goods."

"The Negro race would be much stronger if there were more who could see the benefit of a college education, be it in the professional line or in a trade. I think the higher education of the Negro race will tend towards reducing race prejudice."

'1' The Negro must be an active voter.

'2: He must be encouraged to engage in what he is by nature fitted to follow, this not to be determined by one man or set of men but by the individual.

"3. He should study the conditions of his community and enter such activities as he can. He should strive to establish himself in every line of business possible.

"4. He should study mining and manufacturing. He should become an intelligent farmer, vegetable raiser and cotton producer.

"5. He should be more thoroly grounded in mechanics that he may become an inventor. Our colleges could look out for this. There should be no cheap course in mechanics.

"6. Our schools and other institutions should teach everything that is necessary to make the pupils serviceable and life enjoyable.

"7. The Negro should be urged to contend peaceably and earnestly for everything that is needed to make him a man."

"The Negro is passing thru a critical period of his existence in America and no one can say with certainty what the result will be. To my mind, however, it is clear that he will come out with a loss of political power and interest, but greatly strengthened in wealth, intelligence and manhood which will ultimately force political recognition and consideration and the full enjoyment of his civil rights. The Negro is undergoing a refining and hardening process which tho humiliating and painful will in the end make him stronger and better and will prove a blessing to him, and to his posterity."

"If the Negro is given protection and an equal opportunity in the industrial world he will succeed as a race."

"I think that with better rural schools, longer terms, better teachers, a more practical education for the masses and a higher and more thoro education for the leaders, more effective and aggressive religious training with a practical religion that we live and not simply talk and shout, we shall ultimately build for ourselves character and accumulate wealth, a combination which merits and demands respect. This done the future will take care of itself."

"I believe the Negro should secure all the training the American school system, public and private, can give. He should then enter some occupation, business or professional, for which he seems fitted individually regardless of tradition or prejudice. As he labors he should link himself to every movement for the betterment of the social and economic life of the community in which he casts his lot. He should preserve a manly, courageous attitude on all questions pertaining to the future of his race to the end that the traditions and ideals of his people become a significant and serviceable factor in American civilization. He must seek to show that his uplift, political, social and religious, is necessary to the progress of all America."

"The Negro should occupy and improve every worthy position attainable. In a manly and honorable way he should protest against any racial discrimination shown against him. He should study carefully his white neighbor and strive in every honest way to live in harmony with him. He should qualify himself politically as well as otherwise and become interested in all questions affecting humanity in general and himself in particular."

"The ideal must be reached after: not on the basis of color or race or any such physical divisions or distinctions, but on the basis of humanity. Only by the way of frank, full, free opportunities can we hope for the ideal. The Negro American must be accorded absolute social and political equality and all the rights guaranteed under a pure democracy. "

"All kinds of activities are essential to the growth and proper development of a people. Diversification in education and pursuit is necessary if a people is to be of the highest good to the country."

"Strong, well-trained leadership for the masses. Educational opportunities unrestricted for all as the case may demand. Retention of the right of suffrage and the display of more independence in the matter of voting. A better trained ministry to inculcate sound moral teaching. The organizing in cities of clubs for civic improvement and for demanding better grammar school training for Negro children and for teaching the masses, as far as possible, the proper meaning and duties of citizenship.

Encouraging business enterprises. Vigorously opposing the doctrine of servility and submission—but not service. Co-operation as far as possible and wherever warranted with fair and right-minded whites for civic improvement."

"If the Negro is given a chance and equal rights as a citizen he will eventually climb as high and accomplish as much as any race or people has accomplished. A college training is not bad for him nor does it unfit him for usefulness as is often said; but he is better able to meet the demands and responsibilities of the times."

"In spite of the evidences of prejudice everywhere in our country, I believe that the Negro will some day become a big factor in the political life of the nation and occupy an enviable place in the economic development of the United States. He has already made a marvelous record— a record that should give every man with Negro blood in his veins the highest hope for the future."

"I believe that the American Negro must live and die in America. Africa is not his home for he would be an absolute stranger there. I believe in the ultimate triumph of right. I believe that we will receive our rights and be given full citizenship when we as a people demand the same and not until then."

"If the Negro will be wise and educate himself in the trades and the professions, get homes and own land and build up a strong moral character, he will eventually come into his own and be fully recognized as an American citizen."

"The Negro must work and fight and fight and work. He must scorn peace earned at the price of his self-respect. He must deport himself as a man and he must insist on being treated as a man in America. Much time must be given to the bettering of his environment so that he can will to his children far better surroundings than he himself has inherited. Finally, he must cultivate more of the religion of self-respect and less of the religion of fear."

"The Negro should be given every opportunity and encouraged to get the very best education possible—college education in every possible case before entering a professional school. I think Negroes should enter professions and trades, after college, as their tastes lead them and wherever there is likely to be a demand for such professions and trades. They should own homes and acquire additional property as much as they can. They should have a better educated ministry and more thoroly trained teachers."

"I think that full political rights and a more modified social code may be inaugurated in the future. These higher attainments are not possible until the Negro catches the true spirit of the commercial age in which he lives and lays an economic substructure as his foundation. We must produce a substantial capitalist class. Such a state of economy admits of a leisure class. If this leisure class is composed of persons who are cultured, thrifty and energetic I see no reason why full, political rights should not be attained and a widely modified social code substituted for the sham of ignorance under which we are now living. I think education can help ameliorate conditions."

"A leadership more broadly educated. An intelligent and consistent agitation for the securing of our citizenship rights. A manly stand in all things pertaining to civil, social and moral questions. A right-about-face with regard to the matter of the education of the youth of our race; that is, less industrialism and more intelligence."

"I most strenuously urge that our people, all of them, get the best possible training in the best colleges and universities of the country and affiliate with all the forces and organizations making for the moral and religious development of all the people. In the meantime, I would add, encourage in every way possible all the organizations for the material growth of the country."

"Undoubtedly prejudice is increasing rather than diminishing. This has been brought to our minds more forcibly by the passage of the 'grandfather clause' amendment to the constitution of this state. We who are here in Oklahoma feel that colonization has brought it about as much as anything. Wherever our people congregate in large numbers there very soon begins the agitation for disfranchisement. Were it possible for the race to be widely diffused over the United States, so that they might acquire wealth like the so-called superior race, and be found only a few in any one place, there would be no race problem."

"I believe that the acquirement of education and wealth, the teaching of a saner and purer religion, performance of duties and a demand for all our rights under the law will bring a brighter day for the Negro in America."

"I believe that education coupled with a good moral and religious training will be the main factor in the solution of the Negro problem in America."

"I am rather an enthusiast on the return of a goodly portion of the Negroes to Africa as a final solution, by his voluntary and gradual move as he realizes that he can hardly expect to attain to a full measure of citizenship in all that the word implies in this country."

"The Negro will ever remain in America. Citizenship and opportunity will increase as the Negro grows in stability, wealth and intelligence. Prejudice will be forced to abate as slavery recedes and the Negro acquires independence."

"I believe that as the Negro and the white man are educated up to the truth of the legal equality of all men under our American government each will come to see that all must enjoy the same privileges. Neither is yet equal to the occasion. There are few Negroes who are aggressive and demand, and a few philanthropic whites who acknowledge and concede equal opportunities for all men."

"The Negro is growing more assertive and manly. Every day gives us new evidences of the fact that he is becoming more appreciative of his right to life, liberty and property. He is beginning to meet imposition with opposition, even with his life."

"The Negro needs leaders and instructors who will teach that he is a man and therefore must have all the aids to the better life and good citizenship that other men require; that to become a citizen in the true sense he must enjoy the same opportunities and benefits as other citizens."

"The Negro must measure up to the standard of a man in all respects if he hopes to gain what other races have gained. Hence he must be impressed with the necessity of preparing himself. The young Negro must be inspired with reminders of what other Negroes have accomplished. He must be taught not to close the door of hope upon himself, even in thot. He must be made to feel that competency must win, has won."

"To me, the outlook for the Negro race in America is bright or dark owing to the deportment of the Negro himself. If he will make use of the opportunities he has in educating himself, saving his money, acquiring property and in being a law-abiding citizen there is no law that can successfully stop him."

"Let him cease to be a cringing suppliant; assert his manhood intelligently; speak out against unjust discrimination and laws that affect him; demand a competent leadership in pulpit, school training and politics; give his children the highest possible training and repudiate the stigma of being fit only for the workshop; demand the rights guaranteed to citizens by the Constitution; get property; migrate from the South to all parts of the country."

"The Negro came to America not by his own volition and is here to stay. I believe he should contend for all his rights as an American citizen and enter all lines of competition with the other races in this country."

"The Negro in America should be educated just as any other race in America. One phase of education should not be too much emphasized above another. All phases are necessary for the highest realization of any race. Negroes should demand their rights. It is nonsense to expect perfect harmony between two races so situated as the Negroes and whites of America. The day which brings perfect harmony in America must bring at the same time amalgamation."

"Persecution is a friend of progress. The very things that are denied us we shall still want—and we shall supply them ourselves. Whatever community tries to keep the Negro down must stay there with him. The two things indispensible to the Negro's advance are money and education, both of which things are being slowly but surely acquired by individuals and by Negro communities.   I have no doubt that prejudice is growing but I do believe it is a jealous prejudice and an outgrowth of the desire to keep the Negro in a slave's position.''

''I believe that the ultimate solution of the race problem is amalgamation.''

''We ought now to have all the rights and privileges which are guaranteed by the Federal Constitution. We must agitate and fight to the last ditch for them. Nothing is worth having if it is not worth fighting for.''

''With the highest possible training, the acquisition of property and the launching out into all kinds of business enterprises, the Negro in America will succeed and become a mighty power in the affairs of this country.''

''Industry, economy, obedience to all just laws—in short, the same principles which are helpful to any other race; morality, wealth and education being big factors in the solution of our problem; business enterprises of various kinds which will give employment to the average boy and girl of our race, allowing him to aspire to the highest place in the business.''

''The Negro needs simply the proper training and a fair chance in the business world along with a square deal before the law and he will find a way or make one along by the side of America's best citizens. We must insist on a thoro education however. No limited education in any particular will suffice.''

''The Negroes in America will never develop to the extent of their capacity, will never become a great people, not even a free people, until they have political rights equal to the white race. The man who has no political rights has no way of protecting himself and family.''

''While he must give all due attention to his duties, the Negro must not so act now or at any time as to give the impression that he is satisfied to give up even temporarily any of the rights that belong to him as a man. In the present swift revolving scheme of industrial America, the right to vote is paramount.''

''The Negroes ought to have every right guaranteed by the Constitution of the United States. We are American citizens and should accept no treatment that does not apply equally to every other American citizen.''

''The masses should be trained in such a way as to know well their rights and duties as citizens and should be urged to faithfully perform their duties and quietly, firmly, persistently demand their rights. The Negro men who are really qualified to speak should take a bold, manly stand for the race.''

"The future of the Negro in this country will depend upon the kind of training given to the Negro youth. The same kind of training which has made other races great is also necessary to make the Negro race great."

"The Negro must become a part of all the life about him. He must become Americanized in the best and largest sense. He should be led out of the consciousness that he must have anything less than other citizens enjoy. All kinds of education, all forms of wealth and a knowledge of the ways of the American world are his needs for this achievement. Each one of us must refuse to turn from any avenue of life because other men think it is not for Negroes. We must work, think and live independent of the dictates of those who regard us as less than other men. The best of us should give of our means, our time and ourselves to leaven the whole. College-bred Negroes should live these ideas among the masses and teach them to their children."

A careful reading of the above quotations from the replies of the Negro college graduates discloses on the whole a hopeful and encouraging attitude on the part of these educated men and women. Tho hampered by prejudice and its accompanying discriminations as well as by lack of opportunity these men and women are for the most part hopeful of the future of the Negro race in America.

The suggestions which these replies contain fall in the main under the following groups:

1. Equality before the law.
2. Full citizenship rights and privileges.
3. The right to vote.
4. Unrestricted educational opportunities.
5. Well trained leadership.

Indeed these suggestions are not to be ignored nor even treated lightly if we hope to bring the Negroes of America to a higher place in the scale of social values; and that not alone for their own sake but for the sake of the American people as a whole.

Section 18. Conclusion

The conference, in studying the college-bred Negro for the second time, concludes that the work of the Negro college and that of the college-bred Negro American have been of inestimable value.

While a few Negroes were graduated from Northern colleges prior to 1860, the great work began with the Emancipation. The Negro college came in response to the call for teachers for the freedmen and their children. For less than fifty years then the work has been carried forward and that with remarkable results. From the ranks of the college-bred have come many of the teachers and leaders and professional men and women of the Negro race in this country.

The demand for such workers has always been and is now greater than the supply. The educational field is constantly in need of thoroly equipped teachers and leaders. In fact the whole educational system must be built upon the college else the system suffers from the lack of competent leadership and direction. So, too, in business and in the professions: the man of training will ever be the controlling factor.

These statements have a special significance when applied to the life of the eleven million Negroes in America. Not only for them but also for all America, the colleges of this country have done a great service in sending forth these five thousand Negro college graduates; men and women who by precept and by example have been of great service in lifting the moral, the social and the economic tone of the American people.

The College=bred Negro American

Index